AS Government & Politics

The Constitution & Constitutional Reform

Nick Gallop

Advanced TopicMaster

Series editor
Eric Magee

Philip Allan Updates, an imprint of Hodder Education, an Hachette UK company, Market Place, Deddington, Oxfordshire OX15 0SE

Orders

Bookpoint Ltd, 130 Milton Park, Abingdon, Oxfordshire OX14 4SB
tel: 01235 827827
fax: 01235 400401
e-mail: education@bookpoint.co.uk
Lines are open 9.00 a.m.–5.00 p.m., Monday to Saturday, with a 24-hour message answering service. You can also order through the Philip Allan Updates website: www.philipallan.co.uk

ISBN 978-0-340-98720-9

First printed 2011
Impression number 5 4 3 2 1
Year 2015 2014 2013 2012 2011

Printed in Spain

Hachette UK's policy is to use papers that are natural, renewable and recyclable products and made from wood grown in sustainable forests. The logging and manufacturing processes are expected to conform to the environmental regulations of the country of origin.

Contents

Contents

Introduction

The British constitution was once described as being 'as nearly perfect as a human institution can be'. Edward Shils, in his 1972 text 'The Intellectuals and the Power', was referring to a widely acknowledged 'fact': that Britain's constitutional arrangements were ones of supreme efficiency and unparalleled effectiveness.

Yet recent decades have been characterised by the most rapid and radical process of constitutional reform ever witnessed on these shores. Changes have had an impact on almost every aspect of the political process and on the functioning of the state — from the organisation of central, regional and local government to the everyday rights that citizens enjoy.

Exactly when and why Britain fell out of love with its constitution is the subject of intense debate. Reasons given include social and economic pressures in the second half of the last century and what Vernon Bogdanor (2009) explains as 'a striking loss of national self-confidence…reflected in a loss of confidence in our institutions and in our constitutional arrangements'. Yet when calls for a radical overhaul of the traditional constitution gathered pace, they did so without a clear idea of what the new British constitution should look like. As a consequence, the current constitutional arrangements still have the distinct feel of a 'work in progress'.

In spite of this, the transition from a constitutionally radical Labour administration to a historic coalition of the Conservative and Liberal Democrat parties — each pledging allegiance to a new constitutional agreement for Britain — presents a good opportunity to reflect on the nature and scope of recent changes, the architects of reforms and to look forward to what the future holds for the British constitution.

We start by asking whether the UK's constitution worked. Chapter 1 assesses the strengths and weaknesses of the traditional constitution and explores the forces that put its informal arrangements under immense strain. In Chapter 2 Tony Blair, the key architect of New Labour's constitutional reforms, is put under the spotlight. How did radical constitutional reform come to sit alongside the largely risk-free policies of New Labour and was Blair's personal disinterest at the heart of perceived failures? Chapter 3 looks at Gordon Brown. Much was promised but little was delivered. New Labour's 13-year constitutional programme is assessed in its entirety in Chapter 4.

In Chapter 5 we debate whether the British constitution should be codified and the constitutional direction of the coalition government is tackled in Chapter 6.

A range of questions are included at the end of each chapter for you to test your knowledge and develop your skills of analysis and evaluation. Guidance on how to approach these tasks is given, followed by a list of further reading materials.

The UK constitution: did it work?

The constitutional expert Walter Bagehot, in his collection of essays *The English Constitution*, highlights the innate value of many of Britain's constitutional arrangements, not least the relationship between the executive and the legislature: 'the efficient secret of the English Constitution may be described as the close union, the nearly complete fusion, of the executive and legislative powers'.

In fact, the UK's traditional constitutional arrangements are often linked to the very soul of the state itself: cautious evolution and a steady kind of 'stately home' government are seen as being in keeping with Britain's national character. The widely-quoted constitutional expert Anthony King likens Britain's traditional constitution to one of England's great Gothic cathedrals: 'full of clutter…complex and rich in detail but with a basic outline that was clear and unambiguous. Its essential elements were few.'

There is no doubt that the UK's traditional constitution possessed both strength and durability and also, for several centuries, the confidence of its people.

This chapter seeks to evaluate the nature of Britain's traditional constitution and the forces that led to its reform.

What are the main strengths of the UK's traditional constitution?

The traditional constitution of the UK is regarded as being simple and straightforward in its form. The arrangements are often referred to as the **Westminster model** — a form of government which emphasises the efficiency of a sovereign parliament governing with fused executive and legislative powers within a highly centralised political system. Supporters of such relatively extraordinary arrangements identify several key strengths.

The UK's constitution is adaptable and flexible

The adaptability of the UK's constitution is often cited as its principal strength. The uncodified nature of constitutional arrangements in the UK has provided the political system with the flexibility to react to and accommodate changing circumstances and political crises — from the extension of the franchise in the late nineteenth century with its dramatic impact on representation within the House of Commons to enhanced police powers in the wake of recent terrorist acts.

Box 1.1

Key terms: codified and uncodified constitutions

Constitutions seek to establish and define the framework of a state, how it is organised and the regulations, rights and principles that underpin it.

- A codified constitution is set out in a single authoritative document. The US Constitution is codified. It was drawn up at the 1787 Philadelphia Convention and came into force 2 years later following ratification by the 13 member states.
- An uncodified constitution is not necessarily unwritten, just not set out in a single document. Uncodified constitutions are often described as evolutionary in nature, adapting to and embracing changing political circumstances. The UK constitution is referred to as being uncodified — its sources range from statutes (Acts of Parliament) to works of authority which seek to explain the way that it functions. Parts of it — such as conventions (rules that might dictate certain traditional principles) — are unwritten.

Such adaptability illustrates another key feature of the UK constitution — its ability to evolve over time. Unlike the codified constitution of the USA for instance, protected from change by special procedures, major constitutional change in the UK can be made swiftly and by Act of Parliament (see Box 1.2). The traditional constitution's conservative supporters maintain that this ongoing process of evolution, which has taken place over several centuries, has created an organic body of rules which reflects the deepest values and ideals of its people, rather than an outdated and artificial construct created at a specific point in time.

Box 1.2

Gun laws: constitutional change in the USA and UK compared

The escalation of violent crime in the USA has been matched by a steep rise in the number of gun control laws. The National Rifle Association estimates the number of regulations defining where and when guns can be carried, to be well over 20,000 nationwide. Yet the prospect of constitutional change to the Second Amendment of the US Constitution which protects 'the right of the people to keep and bear arms' is remote. The rise in gun-related

Box 1.2 (continued)

violence (in 2004 there were 29,596 gun-related deaths in the USA) has seen more attempts to restrict private gun ownership — rather than simply regulate where guns can be carried (over 80 cases have been filed). Such cases have all been struck down in defence of the constitutional rights of US citizens, most recently by the US Supreme Court in *District of Columbia* v *Heller* (2008) and *McDonald* v *Chicago* (2010).

In the UK, curbs on rights can happen with remarkable speed when deemed necessary. In the wake of the shooting of 16 primary school children and their teacher in the Scottish town of Dunblane in March 1996 came a call for the total ban on the private ownership of handguns. The Snowdrop Appeal, founded by friends of the bereaved families, collected 750,000 petition signatures inside 6 weeks. The Firearms Acts of 1996 and 1997 which followed banned the private ownership of all cartridge ammunition handguns, regardless of calibre. Although the impact of legislation on gun crime is hard to calculate, the Acts have been criticised for causing the almost complete collapse of recreational and competitive target shooting with handguns in the UK.

The UK's constitution results in strong government

A key strength of the UK's traditional constitutional arrangements is the provision of strong, decisive government. According to the principle of parliamentary sovereignty, ultimate political power lies firmly at the centre. Owing to a fusion between the executive and legislature, the arrangements also allow for the existence of a particularly powerful executive branch.

Box 1.3

Parliamentary sovereignty and strong government

The principle of parliamentary sovereignty means that since there is no superior authority to Parliament, strong government is a defining feature of the political process in the UK. The ultimate supremacy of Parliament to legislate as it chooses is most unlike other modern democracies.

- In Germany, the first 20 articles of the constitution set out the structure of the federal government and the basic rights of German citizens. There is no provision for these to be amended in any way.
- The Constitution of the USA confirms in Article VI, Clause 2 that the constitution — not the executive or the legislature — is 'the supreme law of the land'. Constitutional changes are permitted but require support from two-thirds of both Houses of Congress and three-quarters of all states.

Power under these traditional constitutional arrangements was not merely centralised: it was *concentrated*.

Such arrangements are unlike the dispersal of power between the provincial governments of the Netherlands for instance, or the shared sovereignty of the states of the USA. In the UK, the cabinet-led executive dominates the legislative and policy-making programme at every stage — able to enact and implement its political objectives and manifesto commitments with ease.

The UK government is accountable and responsible

The traditional constitutional arrangements also had the favourable consequence of making governments of the day acutely sensitive to public opinion. The penalty of ignoring the will of the people could be profound. Within a two-party system — the product of a first-past-the-post electoral system which sees relatively small shifts in votes exchange government of one party for government of another — a high level of responsiveness to the wishes of the electorate appeared to be the perfect counter-balance to 'strong government'.

Box 1.4

Ministers, judges and 'abuse of power'

The relationship between the judicial and executive branches is often tested to the limit but serves to demonstrate the effective checks that exist within Britain's constitutional arrangements.

In 2006 the *Guardian* reported on an alleged 'abuse of power' when the Home Office refused to grant leave to remain in the UK to nine Afghan men who hijacked a plane in Kabul and forced it to land at Stansted airport.

'The men said they were fleeing the Taliban regime and had commandeered the Boeing 727 in February 2000 because they had no other choice. After holding 156 passengers and crew hostage in what became Britain's longest airport siege, they were jailed at the Old Bailey, but freed on appeal in 2003 after it was ruled that the law about whether they had acted under duress had been wrongly applied.'

While a high court judge ruled that the government should respect the decision of a 2004 immigration panel ruling — that the lives of the men would be at risk if they were sent back to Afghanistan — Tony Blair referred to the ruling as 'an abuse of common sense': 'We can't have a situation in which people who hijack a plane we are not able to deport back to their country.'

Source: adapted from 'Afghans who fled Taliban by hijacking airliner given permission to remain in Britain' by Jeevan Vasagar, *Guardian*, 11 May 2006

© Guardian News & Media Ltd

Alongside this prevailing sense of government accountability sits government responsibility. King notes that 'precisely because British governments knew that they could be, and ultimately would be, held to account, they tended on the whole to behave responsibly'.

Such responsibility is further underpinned by what the constitutional authority A. V. Dicey referred to as one of the 'twin pillars' of the UK's constitution along with parliamentary sovereignty: **the rule of law**. The government may be able to pass, change and manipulate the law. But a breach of the law is a different matter. Ministers whose actions are deemed to be *ultra vires*, or beyond their power, find their decisions overturned in the courts. For instance, when Michael Howard, as home secretary, intervened to increase the sentence of two murderers in 1996 from 8 to 15 years, his verdict was reversed in the courts.

In summary, the traditional constitution was viewed as a thriving blend of processes and principles — evolutionary processes that encouraged limited but pragmatic reforms to the widely supported principles that underpinned it.

When did the UK 'lose patience' with its constitution?

If the durability, coherence and flexibility of the UK's constitutional arrangements were heralded as undeniable strengths, when did such a 'broad political consensus supportive of the constitution and the key institutions of the UK state', as Lynch and Fairclough put it in *UK Government and Politics* (2010), disappear?

Vernon Bogdanor suggests that the domination of the political agenda by socioeconomic issues in the immediate postwar period ensured that 'the constitution played little part in British politics', arguably for longer than it should have. At the heart of this, writes Peter Hennessey, in *The Hidden Wiring*, lay an obstructive sense of deference among the British people towards their constitutional arrangements that bordered upon indifference. Hennessey notes that 'the British...have been profoundly uncurious about the rules under which the hugely important "national game" of politics and government are played' which he puts it down to 'a powerful combination of smugness, insularity and sheer incomprehension'.

However, out of the failure to find effective solutions to Britain's economic difficulties in the 1950s and 1960s emerged growing doubts about whether Britain's institutions were adequate to meet the challenges of the modern

In April 1981 riots erupted in Brixton, an area of South London then characterised by severe socioeconomic problems, high crime rates, high unemployment, low wages and poor housing

world. Such misgivings were aggravated by an apparent loss of national self-confidence in the second half of the twentieth century, during a period when Britons were forced to watch the disintegration of the British empire, the rise of seemingly unsolvable socioeconomic problems and profound cultural shifts, such as mass immigration and a decline in deference, which challenged the status quo.

The crisis of national confidence was accompanied by a sequence of events that tested the existing constitutional arrangements. These episodes challenged the very framework of the state itself and put considerable pressure on the UK's informal and relatively relaxed arrangements.

Centralising forces

The extension of the franchise from the middle of the nineteenth century began a relentless process of accumulation, then consolidation, of power in the hands of organised political parties and their leaders: especially, the leader

22468

of the largest party in the Commons, the British prime minister. This process was at odds with traditional understandings of the distribution of power in the UK and exposed the informality and weakness of arrangements that had formerly underpinned the political process: from party politics in Westminster to scrutiny in Parliament and to the delicate balance of power between central and local government.

- The Conservative government under Thatcher's abolition of the Greater London Council in the mid-1980s and its replacement with metropolitan borough councils changed the entire structure of local politics in the capital by Act of Parliament.
- Taken alongside the premier's refusal to engage growing calls for the devolution of power to the regions of Scotland and Northern Ireland, this process of centralisation was contrary to the delicate balance of constitutional power in the UK.
- Thatcher's style of leadership appeared to undermine the traditional constitution's key principles of responsible, restrained government and gradual, evolutionary change.

European membership

In 1973, along with Ireland and Denmark, the UK 'joined' Europe. Such a move had profound implications for the UK's traditional constitutional arrangements. Arch-eurosceptic Norman Tebbit is not alone in referring to a 'fundamental deception' at the heart of Britain's membership of the European Union (EU) when it comes to the challenge faced by the UK's traditional constitutional arrangements:

> Entry to the European Economic Community was sold in Britain as entry into a trading system, not as a ticket on a train to economic, monetary and political union. In Brussels it was seen as a commitment — an irreversible commitment — to an ever closer union, which was taken there to mean a political union.

The EU is a constitutional entity in its own right with a written constitution in the form of the Treaty of Rome. In spite of the fact that the EU's historical development, its underlying principles, its character and its culture are very different to those of the UK, its impact on the UK's constitutional arrangements has been profound. Despite Margaret Thatcher's 1988 assertion that 'willing and active cooperation between independent and sovereign states is the best way to build a European Community', no area of the UK state — from elections to rights, and from the roles of central, regional and local government to the relationship between the branches of government at the centre — has remained unaffected.

With the principle of parliamentary sovereignty at its core, serious questions arise as to how it continues to be possible for the UK's traditional constitution to adapt to accommodate a supranational organisation which asserts its own sovereignty in key areas of policy and law.

Elective dictatorship

The steady, relentless power shift towards the centre, the consolidation of power in the hands of the prime minister and the seemingly irreversible decay of local government were all but complete by the mid-1970s. In 1974 came a chilling warning that has had a significant impact on constitutional discussion ever since. Pointing to a Labour government 'legitimised' by a minority of the electorate but bent on radical constitutional change, Lord Hailsham, a conservative politician of some experience, warned that the UK's constitutional arrangements had created an 'elective dictatorship'. It justified calls, Hailsham claimed, for a codified constitution to place effective checks on executive power.

Michael Quinlan, former permanent secretary at the Ministry of Defence, in a contribution to *Hutton and Butler: Lifting the Lid on the Workings of Power* (2004) three decades after Hailsham's warning, maintains that an ineffectively checked executive is as much a feature of modern politics as it was in the 1970s. Quinlan raises serious concerns over traditional understandings of, for instance, the restraining hand of the cabinet on prime ministerial power, evidenced during Tony Blair's premiership and beyond:

> Cabinet government of the traditional model has manifestly atrophied over the past seven years, by deliberate neglect, not accident. Should we mind? If a collective cabinet system no longer functions well, and parliament is docile or impotent, we may be nearer to 'elective dictatorship' than when Lord Hailsham coined the phrase a quarter of a century ago.

The growth in prime ministerial power

Rodney Brazier in his text *Constitutional Reform: Reshaping the British Political System* sketches a caricature of Margaret Thatcher's 'imperious premiership' during which she throws off the restraints that guided her predecessors. Through a combination of the heavy use of powers of patronage, the dismissal of ministers who were not 'one of us', a reduction in the authority of the cabinet, an excessive interference in the affairs of the departments of state, an expert manipulation of the press and the crushing of both civil liberties and local government, within just a few years Thatcher had overturned the subtle constitutional balance of powers that had existed for several centuries. Brazier goes on to add:

> As with all good caricatures, there is much truth in that sketch. But even if it were an entirely accurate reflection of Mrs Thatcher's effect on the constitution, that would be a poor basis on which to deconstruct and reconstruct it.

Just as the 'imperious' Thatcher was followed by the 'consensual' Major, so too was the more 'presidential' Blair followed by a prime minister who pledged at the outset to reduce the powers of the prime minister's office. Such a fluctuating base for prime ministerial power not only confirms the well-known claim by Herbert Asquith that 'the office of the prime minister is what its holder chooses and is able to make of it' but reveals that it would not be sensible to be guided by the governmental style of a single premier when reshaping the constitutional arrangements of the state.

However, Tony Benn maintains that the relentless consolidation of power, not merely at governmental level but at prime ministerial level, has overturned previous expectations and conventions that a prime minister governs subject to the consent of Parliament. Now, says Benn: 'a modern Prime Minister controls government like a feudal monarch, exercising Crown powers but dependent on key interests to support the regime'.

Critics of the way that the traditional constitution has been compromised by the growth in prime ministerial power are not confined to the left of the political spectrum. Writing about Tony Blair, Peter Hitchens complains:

> The enormous powers which the current British Prime Minister has chosen to use so aggressively have given him a sort of presidential aura, but it resembles the near-dictatorial French Presidency of Charles de Gaulle far more than the limited, semi-monarchical Presidency of the USA.

The erosion of traditional government

Commentators also point to the 1990s as a period marked by the decline in methods of government formerly seen as hallmarks of the traditional constitution.
- Many central and local government departments, with no specific constitutional protection, had their powers greatly reduced or handed over to **quangos**, thereby undermining traditional constitutional principles of responsible and responsive government.
- The **privatisation** of many publicly owned industries blurred traditional lines of accountability. New regulatory agencies were established but their roles and responsibilities were not clearly understood.

- Allegations of **sleaze** embroiled dozens of MPs and even members of the royal family, resulting in a loss of faith in the political process and the traditional constitutional arrangements that sustained it.

Box 1.5

Key terms

Quangos

The term quango is an acronym for a 'quasi-autonomous non-governmental organisation'. Such bodies were created to perform governmental roles even though they were unelected bodies. Often set up to regulate commercial or service sectors (e.g. regional development agencies), quangos have been criticised as they are not subject to the same levels of scrutiny in the way that they perform their legal duties or spend public money.

Privatisation

The process of transferring an agency, enterprise or service from state ownership to the private sector is known as privatisation. During the 1980s and 1990s, the privatisation of state-run industries such as British Steel, British Gas, British Rail and British Telecom — placing their ownership into the hands of private shareholders — became synonymous with Conservative Party policy. The process has been criticised since privately run bodies are not subject to the same levels of accountability as public bodies.

Sleaze

Sleaze became a particularly widely used term in the media during the 1990s, more often than not prefixed by the word 'Tory'. It had its origins in the large number of Conservative MPs who were alleged to have indulged in inappropriate or disreputable behaviour while in office. The MPs' expenses scandal in recent years reignited sentiments that British politics was still characterised by dishonest behaviour (or sleaze), undermining faith in the constitutional systems that support it.

When tested, the UK constitution was unable to check the steady flow of power from traditional locations into the hands of the executive. Nor was it able to enforce minimum standards of expected behaviour among holders of public office.

In short, the UK's traditional constitutional arrangements proved to be too weak — in the face of successive governments intent upon the accumulation of power — to uphold the underpinning principles of government responsibility, accountability and evolutionary change. Such arrangements have also proved too outdated to be either helpful or useful as the UK attempts to grapple with a modern world populated by imperfect politicians and new supranational systems of government.

Why did the traditional constitution need reforming?

Groups campaigning for a fully written (or codified) constitution claim that the lack of constitutional clarity in Britain has allowed central government far too much unchecked power. As a result of a lack of constitutional safeguards, checks to prevent the government from overturning long-standing arrangements and from trampling on fundamental rights are seen as being insufficient.

Those campaigning for greater constitutional clarity, groups such as Unlock Democracy, maintain that only a written constitution could 'guarantee political equality' and 'regulate the decentralisation of power and the sharing of sovereignty'. An analysis of whether the UK would benefit from codifying its constitutional arrangements is provided in Chapter 5, but for now, we ask why it was felt that the constitution — for all its strengths and weaknesses — was in need of significant reform.

Box 1.6

Did the traditional constitution need reforming?

Yes
- The arrangements lack clarity.
- The level of flexibility makes it open to abuse.
- There is too much power at the centre.
- Checks on government power are weak.
- It does nothing to encourage 'open government'.

No
- Its enduring strength lies in its flexibility.
- It reflects the values and principles of its people.
- It encourages responsible and responsive government.
- It keeps unelected judges out of the political process.
- It makes government highly accountable.

Michael Moran in *Politics and Governance in the UK* identifies three 'sources of constitutional conflict' through which he seeks to explain why reforming the traditional constitutional arrangements was seen as both necessary and inevitable.

There has been a decline of deference

'The British constitution,' says Moran 'was traditionally a deferential constitution', underpinned by a willingness to obey authority without too much question. Ranging from a widely-held belief that certain members of society possessed an innate superiority when it came to matters of state, to a readiness — when the traditional mystique of the aristocracy declined in the second half of the twentieth century — to transfer that esteem to other figures of authority such as the police, 'deference' was an essential component of the UK's traditional constitutional arrangements.

There is evidence — both anecdotal and quantifiable — to suggest that Britain has experienced a decline in deference:

- More people readily admit to being inclined to break a law if they feel that law to be unjust.
- Civil disobedience during protests is far more prevalent.
- 'Aristocrats', rather than championing their noble roots, often seek to hide their heritage and mask their upper-class accents.

This decline has hit the 'dignified' part of the constitution hardest. The monarchy particularly, and MPs generally, have been the subject of recurrent and increasingly widely reported scandals that have undermined the latent authority invested in these institutions by the passage of time — a key feature of the UK's evolving constitution.

There has been a decline of trust

We are more likely to obey the authority of people we trust. Surveys carried out by a wide variety of institutions indicate that while the public's willingness to trust a range of important groups in society is falling, it is politicians who bear the brunt of this decline in trust. Figure 1.1 shows politicians to be trusted by just 13% of the public — the worst figure since this 'Trust in Professions' survey began 26 years ago. Government ministers fare little better at 16%.

The implications for the UK's traditional constitutional arrangements are significant and the growing lack of trust that people have in politicians is regarded as a key factor in the decline in participation — voting and joining a political party, for instance (see Box 1.7). The public's growing lack of enthusiasm for politics, politicians and the political process is undermining principles of accountability through the electoral process — a feature central to maintaining the principles of 'responsible government' that feature so strongly in the UK's traditional constitutional arrangements.

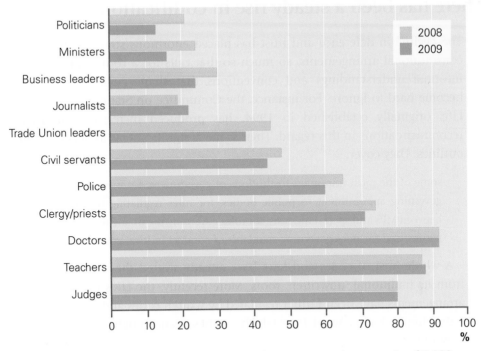

Figure 1.1 Ipsos MORI interviewed a nationally representative sample of 2,023 people aged 15 and over, face-to-face in their homes 4–10 September 2009, asking whether those in the sample thought members of certain professions are 'likely to tell the truth'

Source: Ipsos Mori 'Trust in Professions' annual survey (reported in the *Guardian*, September 2009)

Box 1.7

David Chaytor, MPs' expenses and the decline of trust

In sentencing David Chaytor for fraudulently claiming £20,000 of public money on 7 January 2011, Mr Justice Saunders said the 2009 MPs' expenses scandal had 'shaken public confidence in the legislature and angered the public'. Saunders continued: 'These false claims were made in breach of the high degree of trust placed in MPs to only make legitimate claims. These offences have wider and more important consequences than is to be found in other breach of trust cases. That is the effect they have had and will have in the confidence the public has in politicians.' And striking at the heart of the UK's constitutional arrangements, the judge asserted that MPs' behaviour must be 'entirely honest if public confidence in the parliamentary system and rule of law is to be maintained'.

There has been a steady rise in codification

The decline in deference and trust has placed enormous strain on the UK's constitutional arrangements, so much so that calls for a codification of the informal understandings and conventions that shape political life have become hard to ignore. For instance, the Committee on Standards in Public Life, originally established in 1994, has produced increasingly detailed recommendations in this regard. Their scope is significant, as Michael Moran outlines. They cover:

> some of the most important institutions of government: for more open rules governing appointment to public bodies; for rules regulating the relations between MPs and special interests; for rules governing the financing of political parties; and for rules governing standards of conduct in local government.

A whole host of codes and laws have already shifted the constitution far from its traditional 'unwritten' roots. More recently, the UK's constitutional arrangements have been further regulated by written codes and laws such as:
- the Human Rights Act of 1998 which codifies relations between the citizens and the state
- the Political Parties, Elections and Referendums Act of 2000 which regulates elections and the raising of finance by political parties
- Acts devolving power to the regions which codify the relationship between levels of government in the UK

Conclusion

Few constitutions are lauded quite so emphatically as the US Constitution. Franklin D. Roosevelt acclaimed his nation's constitutional arrangements as 'the most marvellously elastic compilation of rules of government ever written'. The reality is that most, if not all, come with as many strengths as they do weaknesses.

The traditional constitutional arrangements of the UK are no different and yet over the period of half a century their informal nature proved unable to resist radical shifts and alterations in both the institutions of government and in the political processes that underpinned them — surely, critics maintain, the central purpose of any effective constitution.

The perception of the UK's constitutional arrangements as outdated and inefficient gathered pace throughout the second half of the twentieth century, culminating in the championing of constitutional reform by New Labour — a party with a long history of side-stepping this issue.

Task 1.1

Look at the descriptions of the traditional constitution in this chapter.

1   Explain what is meant by the term 'adaptability' when considering the strengths of the UK's traditional constitution.

2   It is often argued that, although uncodified, effective checks did indeed exist within the traditional constitution. Outline and explain the checks that existed in Britain's traditional constitutional arrangements.

Guidance

1   Questions like this — that require short but well-supported responses — appear in many examinations. You should aim to write around four sentences. Try to construct a clear, precise definition of 'adaptability' — one of the central features of any uncodified constitution. There are significant strengths associated with adaptability. Use the text to identify and exemplify at least one of them, then explain the disadvantages of 'adaptable' constitutions — there is an obvious drawback in comparison with the USA in Box 1.2. Finally, try to expand on why the adaptability of the UK constitution might have fuelled calls to codify it.

2   Constitutional checks relate to the power that one branch of government has over another. Although there is much discussion in the chapter of the accumulation of power in the hands of the executive, there is also discussion of the checks that existed. Look back to the section on government being 'accountable and responsible' and the example in Box 1.4. Try to explain who can check whom and how.

Task 1.2

Read the extract below and answer the questions which follow.

Our discussion begins by explaining why the unwritten UK constitution is unusual. In general the constitution is the text which sets out the fundamental and superior law of the nation. It not only describes the main institutions of the state, but also provides a framework of basic rules which determine the relationship between these institutions. In addition, it will usually provide in outline the legal and non-legal rules and procedures that define the system of central and local government. At the same time, the constitution normally places limits on the exercise of power and sets out the rights and duties of individual citizens. Tom Paine explained that it is the property of a nation, and not of those who exercise government: 'A constitution is a thing antecedent to the government and always distinct therefrom.' In nearly every other state the term constitution refers to this document (or series of documents) which contains the fundamental and superior law of the nation.

Task 1.2 (continued)

The constitution of the United Kingdom is unwritten/uncodified in the sense that it is not contained in any single document. Furthermore a codified constitution as a form of higher order law will generally be entrenched. A specified procedural device (e.g. a referendum or a higher majority plus federal ratification) must be followed to introduce changes, which makes a codified constitution relatively difficult to amend. In contrast to most others, the UK constitution is not entrenched. In consequence, it is relatively flexible, in the sense that any aspect can be changed by way of ordinary legislation and certain aspects can be modified by convention.

Source: extract from the introduction to Peter Leyland's
The Constitution of the United Kingdom (2007)

1 What, according to Peter Leyland, is the purpose of a constitution?
2 What are the main difference between the UK's constitutional arrangements and the constitutional arrangements of most other countries? What are the implications of these differences?

Guidance

1 In many respects the purpose of a constitution is reflected in its functions. Using the first paragraph of the extract, outline these functions and explain the purpose of a constitution. Look back to Box 1.1 too.
2 Look at the second paragraph of the extract and think about how the terms 'entrenchment' and 'codification' link together in the context of a constitution, especially when comparing the constitutions of the UK and USA. You may need to look up the term 'entrenched' in a dictionary of politics or on the internet. Think of what an 'entrenched' position in military terms might be like (well protected on the one hand but difficult to move or alter on the other).

Further reading

- Bogdanor, V. (2008) 'A codified constitution for Britain?' *Politics Review*, Vol. 18, No. 1.
- Brazier, R. (2008) *Constitutional Reform: Reshaping the British Political System*, OUP.
- Leyland, P. (2007) *The Constitution of the United Kingdom*, Hart.
- Moran, M. (2005) *Politics and Governance in the UK*, Palgrave Macmillan.

Blair: a reluctant constitutional reformer?

The Labour government taking office in 1997 had not merely promised new policies. It had also pledged to make wide-ranging changes to the way that Britain was governed. The constitutional reforms that featured in the 1997 Labour election manifesto were so far-reaching that some considered them to represent a 'constitutional revolution'. In spite of the fact that many proposals — such as the incorporation of the European Convention on Human Rights into domestic law, the devolving of power to regions and cities and a Freedom of Information Act — would not have been considered particularly radical in international terms, in Britain the potential for the transformation of the constitution was significant.

However, the extent to which the architects of New Labour were committed to the package of constitutional reforms presented to the electorate in the 1990s has long been the subject of debate. Although such ambitious proposals for change captured the public mood and added substance to New Labour's

Tony Blair following Labour's 1997 general election victory

grand-sounding promises of change, there is much evidence to suggest that Tony Blair himself was one of their least enthusiastic supporters. If true, this would undoubtedly have had major implications for the delivery and execution of the programme of promised constitutional change.

How did the Labour Party under Blair come to support radical reform of the traditional constitution?

It is often said that New Labour was born out of failure and the electoral defeats of the 1980s and early 1990s left an indelible mark on Tony Blair. Perhaps understandably, therefore, the emphasis placed on electoral factors in the Labour Party's renaissance far exceeded that placed on matters of government. Policies were designed with voters in mind and were intended to be inclusive rather than ideological — so much so that the saying 'what works' almost became a mantra for Tony Blair in an era of rapid reinvention.

Several factors combined to ensure that radical reforms to the constitution became an integral part of New Labour's programme in the run-up to the 1997 general election.

John Smith's legacy

A close study of the 1997 Labour manifesto reveals the large number of inoffensive 'pledges with caveats' that lie within. Statements such as 'more spending on education as the cost of unemployment falls' were twinned with sweeping anti-Tory sentiments to create a blend strong enough to steer the Labour Party to a historic landslide electoral victory.

The manifesto also featured some ambitious and specific commitments to make fundamental changes to the constitution. Many of these pledges were inherited from the era of John Smith, the popular Labour leader before Blair:

- It was John Smith who had used a 1993 lecture to the recently established reforming group Charter 88, to pledge the Labour Party to the cause of adapting British law to meeting the requirements of the European Convention on Human Rights.
- John Smith, a Scot and a former minister in the Callaghan government responsible for all the devolution bills of the 1970s, had been particularly devoted to the transference of sovereignty to the regions.

- John Smith announced in 1993 that the party would hold a popular referendum on the issue of electoral reform.
- Tony Blair inherited these pledges and went on to reaffirm them — 'partly' says Anthony King, 'for the same reasons as Smith and partly as a gesture of loyalty to the memory of his much-loved predecessor'.

Ideological commitments

Most of the proposals connected to constitutional reform sat comfortably with the Labour Party's socialist roots. Promoting democracy, protecting rights, reducing the powers of establishment bodies and challenging the inequalities and vagaries of traditional, uncodified constitutions are all dominant features of the socialist cause.

However, the predominance of the Conservative Party for much of the twentieth century meant that the prevailing view in government was that radical change to the system of government in the UK was neither desirable nor necessary. Additionally, the relatively short phases of Liberal or Labour control had been dominated by other priorities — often of an economic nature.

By the mid-1990s it became clear from all polling data that the Labour Party was not just on course for a sizeable win at the next general election but with the Conservative Party in growing disarray the Labour Party was also likely to hold power for some time. To many supporters of reform within the party's ranks, it was seen as the perfect opportunity to adopt a radical stance and pass legislation to break the Conservative hold on power forever. The unelected, unaccountable and unrepresentative House of Lords and the close concentration of power in the hands of central government were to be prime targets.

Public support

Support for constitutional reform among the public was always seen as 'soft'. Opinion polls revealed that while the constitution was a matter of concern, it was invariably lower down the list of priorities than other more pressing issues.

In the 1990s the Labour Party was not alone in developing policies that would eventually result in the reshaping of the UK constitution. Work was being done by several other organisations, many of them advocating substantial curbs on the power of central government. The profile of organisations demanding reforms to the constitution grew during the 1990s. Such groups were to have a significant impact on Labour Party policies. In particular:

- Support for the Liberal Democrats — long-time advocates of electoral reform — was steadily rising during the 1990s.

- Groups advocating a codified constitution, such as Charter 88, or the enhancement of rights, such as Liberty, were growing in influence.
- The Scottish and Welsh nationalist causes were being supported in far greater numbers than in recent times.

Frustrations in opposition

The Conservative Party's four successive electoral victories in its 18-year stranglehold on power between 1979 and 1997 had led to intense frustration among opposition MPs. This dissatisfaction prompted questions of a constitutionally searching nature, focusing in particular on:

- the effectiveness of an electoral system that in the 1987 general election allowed for the creation of a majority Conservative government in spite of the fact that 68% of the electorate either voted for alternative parties or not at all
- the ruling of the regions from Westminster by a centralised government that in the 1992 general election achieved just 25.6% of the Scottish vote and 28.6% of the Welsh vote

A further feature, that all but cemented constitutional reform within the New Labour programme, was the need for 'clear blue water' between the Labour and the Conservative parties. With explicit pledges to pursue Conservative economic policies, a key area that had traditionally marked the parties apart had been eliminated. By proposing such a radical stance over the modernisation of government in the UK and by advocating the entrenchment of rights and the democratisation of many archaic practices and institutions, New Labour was able to highlight the Conservative Party's attachment to outdated traditions and signpost its own credentials as a reforming party.

Constitutional reform under Blair: did the achievements match the aims?

In the weeks following Labour's second landslide election victory in 2001, William Hague was still holding the reins of what remained of the Conservative Party as it searched for a new leader. Hague pointed to the lowest general election turnout for 100 years and warned that 'people see politics and parliament as remote from their lives'.

Somewhat surprisingly, Hague's comment came hard on the heels of the most intense period of constitutional activity that the UK had seen in a century. The programme of change undertaken by the Labour government had sought to forge a new union between the people and the political process: between citizens and their government. The extent to which the wide-ranging aspirations for reform were achieved under Tony Blair's leadership is open to debate.

Several of the Labour Party's achievements in constitutional terms — such as the process of devolution and the impact of the Human Rights Act — are analysed in greater depth in later chapters. It is important however to establish the principles behind the party's programme of constitutional change. Commentators suggest that several coherent themes can be identified.

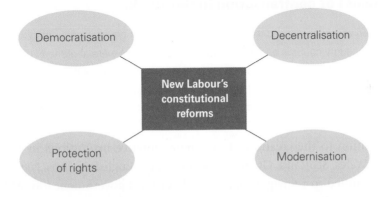

Figure 2.1 New Labour's constitutional reforms

Box 2.1

Labour's constitutional promises

The 1997 Labour Party manifesto contained a number of central constitutional aims. The party promised:

- the holding of referendums prior to the establishment of devolved assemblies in Scotland and Wales, and in London prior to the creation of a directly elected authority and a city mayor
- the holding of referendums on the voting system for Westminster elections and on whether to join the European single currency, and the adoption of alternative electoral systems for devolved bodies
- the removal of hereditary peers from the legislative process, proposals for reform of the House of Lords and new Commons committees to review procedures
- the incorporation of the European Convention on Human Rights into British domestic law and the drafting of a new Freedom of Information Act

Delivering a decentralised state

Aims

The experience of being forced to watch helplessly from the opposition benches as power drained from local government throughout the 1980s had a profound impact on the Labour Party. As a result, the reversal of this process of centralisation became something of a *cause célèbre* among Labour Party members in the 1990s.

Box 2.2

The process of centralisation in the 1980s

Centralisation of power reached its peak under the Thatcher governments when the metropolitan county councils and the Greater London Council were abolished (1986). The remaining local authorities were brought under tighter central control (the semi-autonomous government in Northern Ireland had already been 'suspended' in 1972).

Source: *The Changing Constitution* by K. Harrison and T. Boyd (2006)

In addition to the creation of new representative institutions in Northern Ireland, Wales, Scotland, Greater London and the English regions, New Labour was committed to reinvigorating the role of local government too. Although the proposed dispersal of power stopped short of the creation of a 'federal state' as some commentators suggested, the plans heralded a fundamental restructuring of the British constitution.

Achievements

Perhaps the crowning achievement of New Labour's constitutional reforms was the establishment of the devolved assemblies. Within a year of the 'yes' votes in the 1997 devolution referendums, Scotland and Wales both had their own representative assemblies:

- The Scottish Parliament had tax varying powers of up to 3% and primary legislative powers over major policy areas such as health, education and local government.
- The Welsh Assembly had no powers to vary tax and only executive and secondary (not primary) legislative powers — it can only determine how legislation passed by Westminster should be interpreted in Wales.
- Northern Ireland, following a referendum which ratified the 1998 Good Friday Agreement, saw the creation of a representative body with legislative powers similar in scope to those of the Scottish Parliament.

- The Greater London Authority with a directly elected mayor was created in 1999.

The saying that 'devolution is a process not an event' certainly rings true where the asymmetric transferral of power in the UK is concerned. Just as the regional assemblies had different structures and powers, so too do local governments. While London has an executive mayor with substantial power over environment and transport policy in the capital, only 12 other local authorities in England had directly elected mayors by 2009.

The criticism that New Labour's constitutional reforms lacked coherence is often levelled at the process of devolution. While it has had the effect of transforming the 'Westminster model' into a modern, multi-level system of government, it has also proved costly, has resulted in the unequal provision of services and, in some policy areas with so many different layers of government, has created confusion over accountability and responsibility. In addition, the Labour proposal to create elected regional assemblies in England was scrapped after an emphatic 'no' vote was recorded in the first regional referendum in the North East in 2004.

Box 2.3

Devolution and the West Lothian question

What is the West Lothian question?

The devolution of power to the regions created an anomalous situation. MPs representing constituencies in Scotland, Wales and Northern Ireland are still able to vote in the House of Commons on issues such as healthcare, crime and education, which have no effect on their own constituents. The question was so-called after Tam Dalyell (MP for the Scottish constituency of West Lothian) raised the matter in Parliament, asking:

> For how long will English constituencies and English Honourable members tolerate ... at least 119 Honourable Members from Scotland, Wales and Northern Ireland exercising an important, and probably often decisive, effect on English politics while they themselves have no say in the same matters in Scotland, Wales and Northern Ireland?

Why does it matter?

In recent years several controversial pieces of legislation have found their way onto the statute book with the assistance of Scottish Labour MPs whose constituents are entirely unaffected by the measures. Legislation relating to university tuition fees (which Scottish students would not have to pay) and radical changes to the health service in the form of foundation hospitals (which Scottish patients would not experience) are two beneficiaries of the West Lothian anomaly.

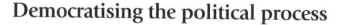
Democratising the political process

Aims

The Labour Party's track record of support for electoral reform has been patchy. However, a key pledge in 1997 was to put the first-past-the-post (FPTP) electoral system used for elections to Westminster under the spotlight. Not only was this notoriously unrepresentative majoritarian system to be voted upon in a referendum but alternative electoral systems were to be introduced for elections to all new assemblies. In addition, Labour's support for electoral reform was underlined by the setting up of an Independent Commission on the Voting System to weigh up arguments for and against FPTP's replacement.

Referendums — once famously described by Clement Attlee as 'alien to our traditions' — were set to become an important part of the political fabric of the UK. The Labour Party was emphatic that all key transferrals of power should be subject to the legitimising effects of referendums. In addition, referendums were promised over electoral reform (for elections to Westminster) and over the adoption of the European single currency.

Table 2.1 Voting systems used in the UK

Electoral system	Use in UK	Key features
First-past-the-post	General elections to the House of Commons	Simple plurality system; single-member constituencies; disproportional outcome.
Supplementary vote	Mayor of London and directly elected mayors	Majoritarian system; used to elect individuals; voters record two preferences; winning candidate has a majority.
Closed regional list	European Parliament elections in Great Britain	Proportional representation system; electors vote for a party in multi-member regions; proportional outcome.
Single transferable vote	Assembly, local and European Parliament elections in Northern Ireland Local government in Scotland	Proportional representation system; electors rank candidates in multi-member constituencies; proportional outcome.
Additional member system	Scottish Parliament Welsh Assembly London Assembly	Mixed electoral system; electors cast two votes — one for a constituency candidate elected by FPTP, one for a regional list candidate elected by PR; list candidates are allocated to parties on a corrective basis to produce a proportional outcome.

Achievements

The creation of the independent Electoral Commission by the Political Parties, Elections and Referendums Act of 2000 was seen as a major step towards establishing controls on electoral spending and the sources of party funds.

New voting systems were adopted in all second-tier elections. The use of these enhanced voter choice and widened the number of parties gaining effective representation. However, although the 'Jenkins Report' — the product of the Independent Commission on the Voting System — had recommended a hybrid electoral system known as alternative vote plus (AV+) to replace FPTP, it was ignored by the newly installed Labour government revelling in its historic parliamentary majority.

In addition, the number of systems currently in use has highlighted the unstructured approach to constitutional reform under Blair, seen as inconsistent at best and confusing at worst. For critics it provides further evidence of New Labour's unwillingness to be truly radical and push for reform of the system used for electing representatives to the UK Parliament at Westminster itself.

Box 2.4

Electoral reform and voter confusion

Evidence for voter disenfranchisement is provided by the 7% (over 140,000) discounted or spoilt votes in the 2007 Scottish parliamentary and local council elections, which prompted Scottish first minister Alex Salmond to protest that 'the decision to conduct an STV election at the same time as a first-past-the-post ballot for the Scottish Parliament was deeply mistaken'.

Source: 'Focus on UK electoral systems', *Politics Review*, Vol. 19, No. 1

Table 2.2 emphasises delivery on the promise of referendums prior to the transferral of power from the centre to the regions. But while referendums have been used increasingly to resolve local issues (e.g. in Edinburgh in 2005 and in Manchester in 2008, over planned congestion charges, and in several cities on the creation of directly elected mayors), on key issues of electoral reform and adopting the euro — promised by successive manifestos during Blair's premiership — referendums were never held.

| Table 2.2 | Referendums held during Tony Blair's premiership |

Table 2.2 Referendums held during Tony Blair's premiership

Year	Place	Question	Yes (%)	No (%)	T/O (%)
1997	Scotland	Should Scotland have its own parliament?	74.3	25.7	60.4
		...with tax-varying powers?	63.5	36.5	60.4
1997	Wales	Should Wales have its own assembly?	50.3	49.7	50.1
1998	London	Should London have a directly elected mayor and an assembly?	72.0	28.0	34.0
1998	N. Ireland	Approval of the Good Friday Agreement	71.1	28.9	81.0
2004	North East	Should the North East have a regional assembly?	22.0	78.0	48.0

Modernising government

Aims

Radical reform of Britain's second chamber was a prime target of many of the Labour Party's most ardent supporters. The Labour Party had felt the injustices of the inbuilt Conservative majority keenly and the removal of the voting rights of the largely Conservative hereditary peers was to be closely followed by a complete overhaul of the House of Lords, including the possibility of a fully elected second chamber.

The House of Commons was similarly not to escape modernisation. Its processes were seen by many as archaic and irrelevant — out of keeping with modern work practices. The setting up of a special select committee to scrutinise its practices was pledged.

Achievements

The House of Lords Act of 1999 confirmed the abolition of the right to vote of all but 92 hereditary peers. Seen as merely the first stage in the process of reform, the upper chamber was left without an overall Conservative majority, awaiting detailed plans for its final form. Proposals were mooted, debated and rejected over the next decade, culminating in a 2007 scheme — voted for by Conservative MPs set upon supporting the most radical (and therefore least manageable) proposals — that would see between 80% and 100% of the House directly elected.

Labour's inability to reform the Lords remained one of the party's biggest disappointments. While reforms to the second chamber in 1999 went some way towards achieving the proposals made in the 1997 manifesto, the designs — as set out two manifestos later in 2005 — to create a 'more representative and democratic' chamber failed to move the process on at all. In fact, such vague pledges illustrated the fact that the party had run out of energy and ideas to resolve the future of the second chamber.

Box 2.5

Ten years of Lords reform, 1997–2007

1997 Labour election manifesto proposes to remove the voting rights of hereditary peers

1999 House of Lords Act removes the voting rights of hereditary peers but under the Weatherill Amendment 92 hereditary peers remain in a 'transitional house'

1999 Government establishes the Royal Commission on Reform of the House of Lords (the Wakeham Commission) in January which makes 132 recommendations on Lords reform

2000 Non-statutory House of Lords Appointments Commission established to nominate cross-bench members and vet recommendations put forward by political parties

2001 Labour election manifesto states that the government will complete the second stage of House of Lords reform by implementing the conclusions of the Royal Commission on the Reform of the House of Lords

2001 Government publishes a White Paper, *The House of Lords: Completing the Reform,* proposing the removal of the remaining hereditary peers, and a majority appointed House of Lords

2002 Joint Committee on House of Lords Reform established, in the words of the then leader of the House, Robin Cook, 'in the hope we can forge the broadest possible parliamentary consensus on the way forward'; all options rejected

2003 Government issues a consultation paper on removing the remaining hereditary peers and establishing a statutory House of Lords Appointments Commission. Bill announced to bring these proposals into effect in the 2003 Queen's Speech but never published

2005 Labour manifesto commits to a 'more representative and democratic' chamber

2006 Joint Committee on Conventions publishes its report, *Conventions of the UK Parliament.* The Queen's Speech at the opening of the 2006–07 session includes a commitment from the government to 'work to build a consensus on reform of the House of Lords and bring forward proposals'

2007 White Paper, *The House of Lords: Reform,* presents both principles and options for the next stage. Jack Straw's 50/50 elected/appointed split is rejected in favour of 80/20 split or 100% elected

Source: adapted from Parliament and Constitution Centre, House of Lords Reform: the 2008 White Paper and developments to April 2010

Under the Blair premiership, reforms to the House of Commons were a similar source of disappointment to modernisers in the Labour Party's ranks — some commentators even referred to pledges on Commons reform as being 'stillborn'. The reforms that did take place were ones of *style* (e.g. the switching of Prime Minister's Questions from two short sessions to one longer one) or *detail* (e.g. enhanced facilities and secretarial support for MPs) rather than *substance* — ones that would make a meaningful impact on the power and influence of the Commons. Perhaps the only truly significant reform was one forced on the leadership from the backbenches: that membership of departmental select committees should be decided by MPs alone and not party whips.

However, a further reform to the institutions of government occurred in 2003 — 'without warning' and without Tony Blair even consulting his cabinet, according to the *Observer*. Although the role of Lord Chancellor had long been criticised for spanning all three branches of government (its holder was a member of cabinet, speaker in the House of Lords and the most senior member of the judiciary) it was the oldest political position in the UK.

Under Blair, the Constitutional Reform Act of 2005 radically restructured the judiciary by removing the judicial role of the House of Lords and creating a separate Supreme Court. It also split the Lord Chancellor's role — handing its judicial appointments role to a separate, independent panel (while retaining the title for the head of the new Ministry of Justice).

A significant criticism of the constitutional reforms under Blair focuses on the fact that some particularly important ones appeared to have been rushed through without proper consideration of the implications. The restructuring of the role of the judiciary, although complete by 2010, was still very much a work in progress from the time of its announcement in 2003 to Blair's departure over 4 years later.

Enhancing and protecting rights

Aims

Pledges on enhancing and protecting rights were twofold. The Labour Party committed itself to incorporating the European Convention on Human Rights (ECHR) in British law and to the drawing up of a Freedom of Information Act.

The Human Rights Act was seen as an opportunity to bring the UK in line with Europe. It was also hoped that by enacting it, the number of embarrassing, though not legally binding, rulings made by the European Court of Human Rights against British governments (over 50 since the mid-1960s) would decline.

On freedom of information, the Labour Party's 1997 pledge stated that 'unnecessary secrecy in government leads to arrogance…and defective policy decisions. We are pledged to a Freedom of Information Act, leading to more open government.' In opposition, the Labour Party gained significant political capital from the allegations of sleaze that dogged the Conservative Party and committed itself — in contrast to the Conservative Party — to open, transparent government.

Achievements

With the passage of the Human Rights Act in 1998, British citizens were finally endowed with the kind of rights that people in other modern democratic states had taken for granted for decades. Rights to life, liberty, a fair trial and freedom of expression and association and from torture or discrimination were just a handful of key rights now enshrined in British law.

Box 2.6

Key provisions of the Human Rights Act

- Parliament and all devolved assemblies must do their utmost to ensure that all legislation is compatible with the ECHR. Judges in UK courts can declare legislation 'incompatible'. If they do, ministers must decide whether to amend the law or appeal against the decision.
- Public authorities — such as government departments or agencies, or the police — who breach rights laid down by the ECHR are now also in breach of UK law.
- Members of the public who feel that their rights have been infringed can have their cases heard in UK courts by British judges, rather than by the European Court of Human Rights in Strasbourg.

However, the Human Rights Act has been the subject of intense political debate. On the one hand, the Act has clarified the roles and responsibilities of the government and state with regard to the rights and liberties of its citizens. On the other hand, it has provoked anger by appearing to facilitate the claiming of damages by prisoners, the prevention of hijackers from deportation and the protection of errant celebrities or public figures from legitimate exposure.

The Act has struck at the heart of the constitutional principle of parliamentary sovereignty by allowing British judges to rule that legislation passed by Parliament contravenes the Act and is therefore unlawful. Under Blair, the Anti-Terrorism, Crime and Security Act of 2001 was replaced with the Prevention of Terrorism Act in 2005 after judges ruled that indefinite detention without charge discriminated against foreign nationals, even if they were suspected of terrorist activity.

As for freedom of information, by December 1997 a White Paper had set out some radical proposals which stated that only information which could result in 'substantial harm' would be exempt from a forthcoming Act. However, after the sacking of the minister responsible for the paper, the eventual Freedom of Information Act of 2000 was significantly altered. Not only was it seen as a 'deep disappointment', according to the Campaign for Freedom of Information, which would do little to improve the openness of government but it would also not come into force until January 2005.

For many, the Labour government proved to be far less keen on radical reform in *office* than it had been in *opposition*.

Blair's constitutional legacy: a lack of vision?

Having reflected on the aims and achievements of the Labour Party's constitutional reforms, two questions remain:
● How wedded was Tony Blair himself to these radical proposals?
● If relatively indifferent, what impact did his lack of enthusiasm have on the implementation of these aims?

According to many commentators, the programme of constitutional reform was indeed adopted by Tony Blair 'without enthusiasm'. In the words of Peter Riddell (2005), the introduction of elected bodies in Scotland, Wales and London, a Human Rights Act and freedom of information legislation were all seen by Tony Blair and his New Labour team as: '…peripheral to his main strategy and Blair seldom highlighted them publicly. When he did refer to these proposals, it was invariably under the label of 'modernisation' rather than pluralism, a deliberate sharing of power.'

Other critics of Blair's approach to constitutional reform, such as Philip Norton, blame the lack of coherence on the then prime minister's reluctance to engage intellectually with the process of constitutional change. According to Norton, constitutional reform was not something that Tony Blair:

> delivered speeches on or…discussed with colleagues and journalists. He was willing to address particular problems, such as resolving conflict in Northern Ireland, but showed no inclination to stand back and locate his actions within a developed and intellectually coherent view of the type of constitution that he thought appropriate for the UK.

Stark contrasts have been made between Tony Blair and the Labour leaders that preceded and succeeded him. John Smith was energised by the process of constitutional change and so too was Gordon Brown — both as chancellor and as prime minister. And it was Gordon Brown who was to place his stamp on the constitution of the UK within less than a month of taking office.

Two examples of Blair's attitude to the programme of constitutional reform serve to illustrate his level of commitment.

Devolution: a distraction from New Labour's prime focus

When Tony Blair assumed the Labour leadership following the sudden death of John Smith, many of his close colleagues were keen for him to drop some of the more emphatic pledges concerning constitutional reform. For example, senior voices such as Jack Straw saw the fraught subject of devolution as 'unfinished business' from the bleak era of the 1970s. Not only had devolution proved to be a key contributory factor in the downfall of that Labour government but it also presented a distraction to New Labour's focus on the economy and improving public services. Anthony King maintains that 'Blair, Smith's successor as Labour leader, simply fell heir to Smith's pro-devolution commitments'.

However, while some senior Labour figures maintained that devolution was not a significant enough issue to the English electorate to devote crucial early parliamentary time to, in his first biography on the Labour leader, Anthony Seldon suggests that: 'Blair's senior Scottish colleagues — Brown, Cook, Dewar and George Robertson — made it clear that they would never allow it to be dropped; and the Liberal Democrats, whom Blair was courting, were also very keen.'

With the Scottish Labour Party unanimously committed to the creation of a Scottish Parliament, devolution stayed, though unlike Smith, Blair retained it for pragmatic political reasons rather than any deep-rooted ideological ones — and with the specific mention of a referendum in the draft manifesto so that any perceived 'break up' of the union would be by the will of the people alone.

Reforming the Lords: 'bored rigid'

Blair's attitude to the reform of the House of Lords is perhaps symptomatic of his relative lack of interest in the programme of constitutional reform. In Seldon's second biography, *Blair Unbound*, he relates that the prime minister's reluctance to embrace constitutional reform was of a personal nature:

'He was bored absolutely rigid by it,' said one aide. 'Supremely uninterested in the details,' said a senior official. So when a victorious Blair returning to Number 10 [in 2001] was presented with a draft bill ready to be introduced into the first session, he groaned, and gave it no priority.

In fact, the future of Lords reform was placed in the hands of the unlikely coupling of Lord Derry Irvine, Blair's former mentor, and the radical — at least by New Labour standards — leader of the House, Robin Cook. From this awkward partnership emerged a rapidly disowned 2001 White Paper followed by the rejection of all five proposals of a 2002 Joint Committee of both Houses. Many commentators are in accord that had Blair only given a lead, reform to the House of Lords could have been achieved in the second term.

Second term blues

Tony Blair's critics within the Labour Party often contrast the achievements of the first term — from the launching of the ambitious programme of constitutional reform to the introduction of a national minimum wage — with the divisions of the second: Iraq, foundation hospitals, tuition fees, stalled reform of the House of Lords. For them, such a disparity lays bare the lack of clarity and ideology at the heart of New Labour, particularly where constitutional reform is concerned.

Many senior figures in the party such as Robin Cook and Stephen Byers were impatient as early as 2001 at the perceived lack of 'radicalism' in the Blair administration — both of them agreeing on, in Cook's words, 'the urgent need to restore to Labour some radical spirit'.

To understand why constitutional reform stalled, one must understand something of the mind of Tony Blair. Seldon reveals that:

> Blair was no more interested in constitutional reform than in 'management'. Neither set him alight. Most of the major constitutional issues, notably devolution to Scotland and Wales and human rights, had been resolved in his first term....Second-term battles can be divided into those about which Blair did not care (House of Lords reform); those he did, but would not fight over (elected mayors); those on which he was prepared to fight hard but accept defeat (the Euro); and those on which he was prepared to fight to the death (Iraq, tuition fees and foundation hospitals).

The final years of Blair's premiership appeared to be dogged by either indecision or ambivalence or both. Indecision lay over exactly what kind of constitution Blair and his team wanted — one that shared certain powers with devolved bodies but not one that diluted government clout by scrapping first-past-the-post. Ambivalence lay over the final destination of the constitution itself: after 10 years in power, the number of unanswered constitutional questions of a programme that lay at the heart of New Labour for a decade is striking.

Conclusion

For many, the irony of the Blair premiership is that the most lasting legacy is the one in which Tony Blair himself showed possibly the least interest — constitutional reform.

Under Blair, Britain saw major changes to both government and the shape of the Westminster model, to the relationship between central, regional and local government and to the courts, judges and rights. While such a lack of interest was less significant in the first term — since much had been planned during the opposition years — in the second term, Blair's disinterest became a significant factor in the progressively more disjointed process of constitutional reform.

Box 2.7

Was Blair a reluctant constitutional reformer?

Yes
- Many of the major ideas were not his own.
- Electoral reform was championed but never got off the ground.
- Reforms to the House of Lords ran out of steam.
- Devolution to the regions was not carried out in England.

No
- The Human Rights Act was radical and decisive.
- Sweeping away all but 92 hereditary peers was radical and created a much more authoritative second chamber.
- Devolution to the regions of Scotland and Wales and the settlement in Northern Ireland were without parallel in history.
- Alternative, more representative electoral systems were brought in for non-Westminster elections.

Task 2.1

1 Copy and complete the chart below.

Theme	Reform	Example(s)	Success?
Democratisation			
Modernisation			
Decentralisation			
Rights			

Guidance

1 Try to ensure that all the necessary detail fits into the chart — especially the two columns on the right-hand side which need to be as detailed as possible. Go back over the chapter and reflect on what the key constitutional reforms were and the extent to which they were achieved. Refer back to and add to the chart as you work through the next two chapters. Use this chart when you are revising.

Task 2.2

Read the extract below and answer the questions which follow.

Constitutional reform is the greatest single legacy of the Blair government. The tidal wave of reforms in the first term released second and third waves which are still working their ways through the system. These secondary waves included further big changes in devolution (in Wales, Scotland and London), in Lords reform, and electoral reform, and in the changes flowing from the Human Rights Act and the new Supreme Court. This second wave needs a strong narrative to explain the need for continuing reform, which works at the constitutional level and at the level of the individual citizen.

[However]…it is one of the great paradoxes of the Blair government that the Prime Minister is famously uninterested in constitutional reform. In his mind it was the

Task 2.2 (continued)

agenda in the first part of his term, when the government legislated for devolution, the Human Rights Act and Lords reform stage one. After that they moved on to the bread and butter issues of education, health, crime, etc. The irony is that constitutional reform will be seen as the greatest single legacy of the Blair government. It continued into the second term, and…it continues strongly still. Constitutional reform generates a powerful political, legal, and institutional dynamic, with further big changes still to come.

Source: adapted from 'The continuing dynamism of constitutional reform' by Robert Hazell, *Parliamentary Affairs*, Vol. 60, No. 1

Reproduced by permission of Oxford University Press

1 Why does the extract suggest that there is 'irony' surrounding Tony Blair's constitutional reforms?

2 Identify and explain two factors which might explain Tony Blair's lack of commitment to constitutional reform.

Guidance

1 Look carefully at the reference to 'irony' in the second paragraph. Try to construct a short paragraph which balances aims, achievements and Blair's attitude to constitutional reform.

2 Look back at the final section of Chapter 2 — 'Blair's constitutional legacy: a lack of vision?' Pick out the key points which seek to explain why Tony Blair might have steered clear of key constitutional reforms.

Further reading

- Charter 88: www.unlockdemocracy.org.uk
- Hazell, R. (2007) 'The continuing dynamism of constitutional reform', *Parliamentary Affairs*, Vol. 60, No. 1.
- King, A. (2007) *The British Constitution*, OUP.
- Riddell, P. (2005) *The Unfulfilled Prime Minister*, Politico's.
- Seldon, A., Snowdon, P. and Collings, D. (2007) *Blair Unbound*, Simon & Schuster.

Brown: a failed constitutional reformer?

Unlike Tony Blair, constitutional reform had often featured prominently in the political rhetoric of Gordon Brown. In fact, Brown's first speech in the House of Commons as prime minister dealt exclusively with constitutional issues when, in July 2007, he declared his intention to make the British government a 'better servant of the people'. Parliament, Brown had said, was to be given a far greater role over a whole range of new areas — from approving public appointments and declarations of war to scrutinising the national security strategy. The UK's citizens were to be given a new constitutional deal as the prime minister pledged 'to bring government closer to the people'.

This chapter assesses Brown's goals, his successes and limitations in the arena of constitutional reform.

Gordon Brown, the new Labour prime minister, speaking in the House of Commons in 2007

Did Brown promise a constitutional settlement at last?

Just a month after Gordon Brown's accession to Number 10 came the publication of a Green Paper, *The Governance of Britain*, in July 2007. Hailed as Gordon Brown's blueprint for the future of the UK's constitution (though the prime minister himself referred to it as less of a 'final blueprint' and more of a 'route map' towards change), it put the spotlight back on the promises that New Labour had made to the electorate 10 years before.

The Governance of Britain was seen as a genuine attempt to revitalise the process of constitutional reform (see Box 3.1) and to conclude unfinished business, such as Lords reform and further entrenching rights. But alongside many other pledges, the main objective of the Green Paper was clear: there was to be a radical reduction in the power of the executive. Brown's Green Paper had four clear targets:

- limiting the powers of the executive
- making the executive more accountable
- reinvigorating democracy
- Britain's future: the citizen and the state

Box 3.1

The Governance of Britain

Our constitutional arrangements fundamentally underpin how we function as a nation. The nature of the relationship the Government has with citizens, the credibility of our institutions, and the rights and responsibilities of citizens all determine the health of our democracy.

Without a shared national purpose, and a strong bond between people and government, we cannot meet the challenges of today's world — whether in guaranteeing security, delivering world class education and health services, building strong communities, or responding to the challenges of globalisation.

Source: extract from the foreword to *The Governance of Britain*, July 2007 (CM 7170, 2007), by Gordon Brown and justice secretary Jack Straw

---

The Governance of Britain conceded that in spite of a decade of constitutional reform by New Labour (of which Gordon Brown was a key architect) 'power remains too centralised and concentrated in government'.

Instead, the Brown government sought to reinvigorate British democracy by clarifying the role of government: finally making people 'proud to participate in decision-making at every level'. But 'we want to go further' said Brown and Straw in their foreword: a 'new relationship' was sought between government and citizens that would 'begin the journey towards a new constitutional settlement — a settlement that entrusts Parliament and the people with more power'.

Limiting the powers of the executive

The most prominent targets of the paper were the powers of the executive, particularly the potent but unchecked prerogative powers which, the paper said, 'should not, in a modern democracy, be exercised exclusively by the executive'. Decisions such as those to:

- deploy troops abroad
- dissolve or recall Parliament
- appoint bishops and judges
- establish rules governing the civil service

were among many powers that would be surrendered by the government or severely limited by legislation.

The relevance of the decision to allow a parliamentary vote on deploying troops abroad was clearly a reaction to Tony Blair's retrospective vote on the unpopular Iraq War and the subsequent failure to find the weapons of mass destruction (the presence of which had been used to justify it).

In addition, the Green Paper also committed the government to:

- working to increase parliamentary scrutiny of some public appointments to ensure that they are appropriately scrutinised

Box 3.2

The role of the Attorney General in the events leading up to the Iraq War

Following continuing pressure and increasing media scrutiny, the Attorney General's full advice on the legality of the war with Iraq was published on 10 Downing Street's website on 28 April 2005. The document showed that the Attorney General's advice of 7 March 2003 had examined possible doubts and arguments about the legality of the war. However, none of these concerns had appeared in the published advice of 17 March 2003. This only served to fuel speculation that Lord Goldsmith had changed his mind on the legality of going to war with Iraq in the face of direct political pressure from Downing Street.

Source: from the *Select Committee on Constitutional Affairs Fifth Report: Recent Controversies Surrounding the Role of the Attorney General*, published in July 2007

- reviewing the role of the Attorney General to ensure that the office retains the public's confidence

Rather like the proposed check on the executive's so-called 'war-making powers', the review of the role of the Attorney General was seen as a reaction to the lack of consistent advice from the Attorney General to the cabinet in the run-up to the Iraq War (see Box 3.2).

Making the executive more accountable

Changes in the area of executive accountability were designed to make the executive more answerable to Parliament and to the people. It was also a bid to make the process of government more transparent and more consultative. Aims included:

- the publishing of a National Security Strategy (to be overseen by a new National Security Committee chaired by the prime minister)
- the introduction of a pre-Queen's Speech consultation process on proposed legislation
- inviting Parliament to hold annual parliamentary debates on the objectives and plans of major government departments
- limiting the pre-release of official statistics to ministers to 24 hours before publication

A further commitment to ensure that government expenditure was reported to Parliament in a more transparent fashion appeared to be a response to criticisms of the Blair governments that the public were being deliberately misled by announcements of the same spending increases several times over.

Reinvigorating democracy

The Governance of Britain revived debate over the composition of the Lords and committed the government to developing reforms for a wholly or substantially elected second chamber. In addition it focused on ensuring that local services and public bodies were more responsive to the people and to the communities that they served.

The paper also proposed a range of strategies designed to encourage participation:

- to consult on moving voting to weekends for general and local elections
- to complete and publish a review of voting systems in line with the government's manifesto commitment
- to review the provisions that govern the right to protest in the vicinity of Parliament

The revival of citizenship

Four key statements asserted that the government:
- would initiate an inclusive process of national debate to develop a British statement of values
- was to work with Lord Goldsmith to conduct a review of British citizenship
- planned the launch of a Youth Citizenship Commission, looking at citizenship education, ceremonies and the possibility of reducing the voting age
- would consult on the current guidance on flying the union flag from government buildings and Westminster Parliament

The plan to encourage a national debate on British values was an interesting feature of the paper which, some said at the time, might at last herald a full Bill of Rights and Duties replacing the Human Rights Act.

In September 2007, just 2 months after the publication of *The Governance of Britain*, Gordon Brown announced the creation of a speaker's conference to grapple with issues such as lowering the voting age to 16 and the use of independent citizens' juries to assist the government in the formulation of policy.

Box 3.3

Citizens' juries

The first citizens' jury was held in Bristol, when a group of students, parents, teachers and community leaders met to discuss education and children's services. Another jury of about 100 people met in Leicester to discuss law and order and a much larger one, of about 1,000 people, was convened in Birmingham, one of nine events across the country to discuss the future of the National Health Service.

Source: 'The constitution under Gordon Brown' by Philip Norton, *Politics Review*, Vol. 17, No. 3

Coherence and direction at last?

The constitutional expert Lord Norton identifies three important ways that Gordon Brown's initial approach to major constitutional reform was different to Tony Blair's and, at the time, had the potential to finally set the UK's arrangements on course for a constitutional settlement.

The proposals were different in scope

Brown's proposals focused more on Parliament — strengthening it as an institution and making it more able to check prerogative powers — while Blair's proposals concentrated on the transferring of powers to new legislative bodies all over the UK. Brown's proposals to deal with the relationships within existing institutions, especially between the executive and Parliament, would be less visible than Blair's and would not result in the creation of new institutions.

The proposals had more coherence

While Brown's proposals still did not offer a clear 'end point' for the constitution of the UK, a clearer overall strategy was more evident than in Blair's package of reforms. The goal was to shift the balance of power away from the executive and towards Parliament and the people. This goal was underpinned by a range of specific proposals that challenged the traditional Westminster model of a dominant executive.

The proposals derived from the personal commitment of the leader

Unlike Tony Blair, who himself showed no real engagement with the issue of constitutional reform and had inherited the vast majority of the party's constitutional pledges from his predecessors, Gordon Brown had reflected personally on the institutions and their roles. Brown had sought to draw together recommendations made by other bodies (such as the Constitution Committee in the Lords) and combine them with his own proposals to create a clear framework for constitutional change.

Conclusions

At its launch, *The Governance of Britain* was not without its critics. Some said that it marginalised key areas, such as electoral reform. Others complained that there were no new proposals for subjecting government bills to more exacting standards of scrutiny and that the areas of scrutiny that were to be 'beefed up' — such as ratifying the deployment of troops abroad — were rare. In addition, some said, many of the key proposals had been suggested before — the Liberal Democrats had already made explicit mention of a War Powers Act and a Civil Service Act, for instance.

In spite of this, it was clear that Parliament was to have powers that it had never held before and in the words of the Hansard Society think-tank: 'Gordon Brown's proposed reforms to make Parliament more accountable to the people are a welcome step towards a strengthened Parliament and a more vibrant representative democracy.'

Commentators waited expectantly for the outcome of the proposed national debate on the UK's constitutional future.

What factors stood in the way of Brown's goals?

In the 1960s when the prime minister, Harold Macmillan, was asked by a journalist what was likely to blow government plans off course he famously responded, 'Events, dear boy, events.' For Gordon Brown as for Macmillan, dramatic and largely unforeseen events were to have a ruinous impact, not only on his programme of constitutional reform but also on his role as prime minister.

The economic crisis

Within a year of Gordon Brown taking office, Britain was struck by a global economic crisis the magnitude of which had not been seen for generations. Likened to the depression of the 1930s which lasted for the best part of a decade, the credit crunch of 2008 sent the financial markets into turmoil and dominated the political landscape for the rest of Brown's premiership.

When the queen announced, in December 2008, that her government's priority was 'to ensure the stability of the British economy during the global economic downturn' many commentators suggested that it was the programme of constitutional reform, most particularly the Constitutional Renewal Bill, that was to become the biggest casualty.

A vague royal reference to proposals being 'taken forward' and a complete lack of specific pledges of a constitutional nature led many to conclude that Brown's early constitutional promises had been supplanted by events. 'Bank bills took precedence,' confirmed Lord Norton succinctly. The imminent collapse of the banking system and the eye-watering levels of government debt led Anthony King to conclude that 'people falling off a cliff seldom devote much time to figuring out how to reconfigure the local topography'.

The expenses scandal

A pre-emptive strike on the integrity of Britain's political representatives came early in 2009 when a *Sunday Times* investigation identified four peers who had declared themselves willing to accept money in return for tabling legislative amendments. But a revival of the programme of Lords reform in the wake of these allegations appeared to have been side-stepped as the justice secretary, Jack Straw, declared that any measures to reassure the public's faith in their ennobled representatives would be independent of a wider programme of Lords reform.

However, the parliamentary expenses scandal that followed, when the *Daily Telegraph* published a list of expense claims made by MPs over several years, caused such widespread public outrage at the perceived abuse of the largely unregulated system of allowances and living expenses that trust in politicians hit an all-time low. Sackings, de-selections, enforced retirements and public apologies abounded as the scandal hit the headlines all over the world.

Needless to say, Brown's constitutional plans were dealt a further blow as the focus of politicians, media commentators and the public alike was set on cleaning up Parliament rather than on the centre–local relationship or the nature of civic engagement. Preoccupied by their response to the crisis, the much-heralded programme of constitutional reform announced in 2007 by Brown's government appeared to have been all but shelved.

The lack of a clear goal

Although unforeseen events contributed to the thwarting of Gordon Brown's constitutional reforms and some proposals originally made in *The Governance of Britain* were revisited, resulting in the creation of a Select Committee on Reform of the House of Commons which made several recommendations to strengthen scrutiny of the government, the main problem lay with the programme of reform itself.

In spite of crediting Gordon Brown with far more intellectual commitment to constitutional reform than Tony Blair, the reforms that moved from Green Paper to draft bill still lacked any real coherence in terms of articulating what kind of constitutional arrangements Britain should be aiming for. Yes, the Westminster model of government, characterised by a largely unchecked executive operating within a heavily centralised state, should be overhauled, but what was the alternative?

How effectively were Brown's goals converted into legislative proposals?

If one criticism of the package of reforms proposed by Gordon Brown was its lack of a clear goal, further disillusionment lay in both the disparate nature of the proposals themselves and in the disappointing exclusions that saw significant areas of reform — to the electoral system and to the Lords for instance — left out completely.

The Constitutional Renewal Bill: disparate

While the original Green Paper had the unchecked powers of the executive firmly in its sights, it also made emphatic statements on a wide range of subjects. From guidelines for the operation of the civil service to a national debate on 'Britishness' and from radical suggestions designed to remedy falling electoral turnout to the creation of new parliamentary committees, the proposals made in 2007 were seen as loosely related at best and incoherent at worst.

However, the Constitutional Renewal Bill did little to add either clarity or coherence to the detail of the original Green Paper. Former head of the civil service, Sir Andrew Turnbull, described it as 'a ragbag of disparate issues' and the joint committee charged with scrutinising the bill found the free-standing themes (see Box 3.4) which spanned three volumes and 266 pages difficult to unify. The committee eventually suggested that renaming it the Constitutional (Miscellaneous Provisions) Bill would have been more appropriate.

Box 3.4

After a lengthy consultation period that elicited over 1,000 responses on five published documents, the bill proposed reforms in six key areas:
- demonstrations in the vicinity of Parliament
- the role of the Attorney General
- the process of judicial appointment
- the war and treaty-making powers of the executive
- the statutory basis of the civil service
- guidance on union flag flying

The Constitutional Renewal Bill: disappointing

Criticisms of the original Green Paper's lack of 'ground-breaking' direction were soon replaced by the realisation that virtually all the truly pressing constitutional issues had now been sidelined in favour of tackling what seemed like marginal or technical ones. Dealing with restrictions on the number of days that the union flag could be flown from public buildings, for instance, seemed utterly inconsequential when compared to reforming the electoral system or creating a British Bill of Rights.

Former Lord Chancellor Lord Falconer was one of the first to launch an attack on the substance of the reforms within weeks of their publication, branding them 'trivial'. Falconer, delivering a withering assessment to the joint committee that was considering the bill, suggested that: 'It is better to describe it as the constitutional retreat bill than a constitutional renewal bill. I believe there is next to nothing of significance [in] this bill.'

With the announcement at the end of 2008 that a constitutional reform bill would be introduced only 'when time allows' during the following parliamentary year, the government signalled that the measures which had formed the bedrock upon which Brown's premiership was built had all but fallen by the wayside. Headline-hitting measures to allow MPs a vote prior to Britain going to war and enhanced scrutiny of treaties had been quietly sidelined.

Any bill to take forward the 2008 Queen's Speech measures was conspicuous by its absence. Recession-fighting measures were where the action was. In 2009, economic — not constitutional — legislation was to be the focus of the government's plans.

Conclusion

On becoming prime minister it seemed as though Gordon Brown — unshackled from the Treasury and liberated from the shadow of the man that had become his nemesis — would finally be able to pursue his own ideological agenda and deliver in the areas that New Labour under Blair had come up disappointingly short on. Brown had clarity and Brown was emphatic. His targets were clear and his proposals direct and unswerving.

And yet just under 2 years later commentators and fellow Labour MPs alike were asking the same question: 'What does Gordon really believe in?'

In 2007 Gordon Brown had called for a sustained public debate on Britain's constitutional future. He had expressed a desire to see all the political parties and all the people of the country 'agree on a new constitutional settlement'. Green Papers and White Papers abounded — on Lords reform, on citizen engagement, on rights and responsibilities, on Scotland's future. But words did not lead to action. Departments of government were largely inactive, the public remained disengaged and the media disinterested in matters of a constitutional nature.

However, in 2009 the expenses scandal, revealed earlier to have all but shelved plans of a constitutional nature, actually began to spark the slow-burning embers of constitutional reform. The summer of 2009 saw Gordon Brown responding to the loss of public confidence and promising that — this time — things would be different: that his government would 'consult widely' and actually 'come forward with proposals'. Little or nothing emerged.

By 2010, and in the run-up to the general election, empty rhetoric took centre stage as there suddenly seemed to be little of constitutional significance that

Gordon Brown did not want to tackle. The Labour Party manifesto, he said, was to 'chart a course' to a written constitution with fixed-term parliaments, voting reform and a solution to the future of the second chamber — all within 'the most comprehensive programme of constitutional reform in this country for a century', said Brown in April 2010.

To his critics, such as Peter Riddell writing in *The Times*, 'Gordon Brown has always been better at talking about constitutional reform than achieving it'. The announcement of support for electoral reform, in the form of the alternative vote, in the dying months of his premiership was seen as characteristic of the Brown approach: 'full of grand commitments', Riddell goes on, 'but his government has dithered for so long that overdue reforms…will not happen before the election'.

Finally, a diary entry on 18 January 2010 by Chris Mullin — former Labour minister and long-time backbencher — in the second volume of his memoirs, *Decline and Fall*, provides a fairly damning conclusion to Gordon Brown's plans for constitutional reform. When considering whether a proposal for a referendum on electoral reform should be contained within the Constitutional Renewal Bill or the manifesto, Mullin comments that: 'If tinkering with the electoral system is such a good idea, we should have done it years ago. Now it's too late and stinks of desperation and self-interest'.

Box 3.5

Seven reasons why Brown is seen as a failed constitutional reformer

1 Electoral reform was left out of the 2007 document *The Governance of Britain* and yet returned to feature prominently in the run-up to the 2010 election.
2 Many of the key features of early suggestions for reform — such as an enhanced parliamentary 'war powers' role — had been suggested by other parties and organisations.
3 A proposed national debate on the future of the UK's constitution failed to materialise.
4 Plans for constitutional reform were shelved in the midst of the economic crisis and yet constitutional failures (elections, non-fixed-term parliaments) were later 'identified' by Brown as being responsible for the 'fundamental rupture in the bond of trust between those who serve, and those who they are sworn to serve' — April 2010.
5 The Constitutional Renewal Bill focused on technicalities or 'trivialities' rather than major issues such as a British Bill of Rights.
6 Many proposed reforms were criticised as they lacked either coherence or a clear goal.
7 Brown returned to radical reforms such as codifying the constitution and changing the electoral system only when facing electoral oblivion in 2010.

Task 3.1

1 Outline and explain three ways that the 2007 Green Paper, *The Governance of Britain*, intended to check the powers of the executive.

2 Outline and explain three factors that hampered Gordon Brown's proposals for constitutional reform.

3 Why was the Constitutional Renewal Bill criticised as being both disparate and disappointing?

Guidance

1 Look back to the first section in this chapter and explain how some of the key targets of the paper would actually check the powers of the executive.

2 Look back to the section entitled 'What factors stood in the way of Brown's goals?' earlier in the chapter. Briefly summarise each of the factors and explain how they might have knocked Brown's reforms off the political agenda.

3 Write a brief explanatory summary of the Constitutional Renewal Bill. Explain, using specific examples, how and why the bill was criticised.

Task 3.2

Read the extract below and answer the questions which follow.

The implications of the expenses scandal

The MPs' expenses farce has destroyed faith in politics and politicians. In attempting to deal with the scandal that they created by over-claiming their expenses, MPs in a blind panic did something quite extraordinary and almost without precedent. They invited in an outside authority — Sir Thomas Legg — to judge their actions and in doing so placed him above Parliament and by extension, the electorate. Until now Parliament had only one auditor: the electorate, in regular elections.

But who elected Sir Thomas Legg? Not a single soul. Yet somehow this crop of MPs made the Commons accountable to him. They have forgotten the point of their existence.

Source: adapted from 'How the rotten Parliament sold our birthright'
by Iain Martin, Wall Street Journal Europe, February 2010

1 On what grounds does Iain Martin suggest that Parliament's response to the expenses scandal was 'extraordinary'?

2 In 'placing him [Sir Thomas Legg] above Parliament' Iain Martin is arguing that a key principle of Britain's constitutional arrangements had been compromised. What was it and why?

Task 3.2 (continued)

Guidance

1 Refer back to Dicey's 'twin pillars' of the constitution mentioned in Chapter 1 — write a brief definition of parliamentary sovereignty.

2 Explain how this principle might have been compromised by the response to the expenses scandal.

Task 3.3

Read the extract below and answer the questions which follow.

15 parliamentary minutes

12:32 'The subject of politics itself has become the focus of our politics,' Brown begins. He intends to rebuild the legitimacy of Parliament. There will also be disciplinary procedures for those who misbehaved. There will be further restrictions on expenses (already agreed by the Commons) but he describes these measures as necessary but insufficient.

12:34 The Commons and Lords will move from self-regulation to statutory regulation. No more can Westminster operate in ways reminiscent of the last century, Brown argues. As part of that process, the new regulator will supervise value for money to make 'Parliament cost less'. There will be a statutory code of conduct for all MPs. It will clearly codify misbehaviour much more clearly. The current system of sanctions is not 'fit for purpose'. The last person to be expelled from the House was 55 years ago, and members can be sent to prison for a year without losing their seat, he mentions.

12:37 The House of Lords: There'll be a review of Lords accountability, cost and transparency, and new laws for disciplinary sanctions for peers. There will be modernisation of the procedures in the Commons, including democratising select committee memberships and allowing more time for non-governmental tabling in the main chamber.

12:39 The first laughs, when Brown says he has made the executive more accountable to Parliament. There will be movement on the following issues: Elected peers in the House of Lords before the summer adjournment. The rights and responsibilities of British citizens will be clarified, potentially through a British constitution. Power will be devolved to local communities, and there will soon be recommendations on devolution in Scotland, Wales and Northern Ireland. The same goes for local government. He defends having a link between an MP and their constituents, but says if there is strong disagreement in the country there

Task 3.3 (continued)

could be movement. 'We will set out proposals for taking this debate forward,' he says, whatever that means. It sounds like not much. There will be action to increase the engagement of young people.

12:43 'In the midst of all the recriminations, let us seize the moment...' He stops to tell the Speaker the House isn't behaving properly. '...to rise to a higher standard. Britain deserves a political system that is equal to the hopes and character of the British people.' Hateful shouts from the opposition. Cameron gets up and mentions how quickly Brown read it. Predictably, Cameron says what we need is a general election. He gets to the proposals. Parliament is too weak, and the government is unwilling to give up power. The Tories support much in the statement because Labour stole it, apparently. 'They have at least mastered the art of copying things.' He calls for regional quangos to be scrapped. Why won't the PM just say today that he'll give up control of select committee membership? He's prepared to do it — is the PM?

12:47 Cameron highlights how often Brown has done this. He did — if you remember — a big constitutional renewal bill when he became PM, and is doing it again now — 'endlessly launched and re-launched.' It's a 're-launch distraction' strategy, Cameron argues. He mocks Brown's constitutional renewal committee, as 'a bunch of ministers talking to themselves'. How do we give power back to the man and woman in the street? Cameron wants citizens' initiatives and a veto on local council tax rises. He wants a referendum on Lisbon, because these anti-democratic moves have sucked out the heart from British politics.

Source: adapted from **www.politics.co.uk.** Ian Dunt reports 'as-it-happens' for 15 parliamentary minutes as Gordon Brown looks to relaunch the Labour Party's constitutional agenda on 10 June 2009

1 What evidence does the author give for the current system of regulating MPs being 'not fit for purpose'?
2 What proposals are made to strengthen Parliament's role?
3 Why do you think that 'the first laughs' followed Brown's assertion that he had made the executive more accountable?
4 What are the two main thrusts of David Cameron's attack on Brown's proposals?

Guidance

1 Look particularly at the first two paragraphs. Is there any evidence that the system is ineffective?
2 Look at the third paragraph. Write down and try to explain the implications of the proposals.

Task 3.3 (continued)

3   Refer back to the main 'target' of Brown's Green Paper *The Governance of Britain*, nearly 2 years before, discussed earlier in the chapter. What was the target of *The Governance of Britain*? What were the criticisms of the Constitutional Renewal Bill? Why might Brown's statement have prompted laughter in the Commons?

4   Look at the final paragraph. Identify the key points raised by Cameron in opposition to Brown's proposals.

Task 3.4

1   Visit **www.parliament.uk** and click on 'Committees' at the right-hand side. Then click on 'All committees A–Z' and find 'Liaison Committee (Commons)'. The page gives a brief overview of the work of the committee and under 'Committee News' you can click on the latest activities of the committee.

2   Find and note down some specific examples of the Liaison Committee holding the executive to account.

Further reading

- Norton, P. (2008) 'The constitution under Gordon Brown', *Politics Review*, Vol. 17, No. 3.
- Seldon, A. (2010) *Brown at 10*, Biteback.
- News and views of a constitutional nature: www.politics.co.uk

Chapter 4

New Labour: a 'new constitutional settlement' for Britain?

The sheer scope of New Labour's reforms makes finding comparatively similar periods of constitutional upheaval remarkably difficult. The list of changes to the constitutional arrangements of the UK made between 1997 and 2010 is as impressive as it is wide ranging. It includes the creation of a supreme court, devolved assemblies, new electoral systems, a reformed House of Lords, freedom of information legislation and statutory human rights. Indeed Professor Peter Hennessey goes back to 1688 — and the Glorious Revolution which enshrined parliamentary powers forever — to locate a suitable comparison to what he terms New Labour's 'extraordinary enterprise'.

And yet the achievements are repeatedly said to lack coherence. The party that enacted them is described as having no 'guiding philosophy' behind permanent and, for the most part irreversible, changes.

So while the reforms are impressive and have brought about a significant rebalancing between the institutions of government and the relationship between citizens and the state, equally 'impressive' are the areas left unreformed or untouched:

- In 2010 Britain still had neither a codified constitution nor a British Bill of Rights.
- The passage of the Human Rights Act does not mean that offending legislation is automatically struck down since the principle of parliamentary sovereignty preserves Parliament's ability to choose whether to amend offending items or not.
- Devolution has been 'asymmetric', meaning that the power and scope of each regional assembly is different and, consequently, the levels of public services provided are different too.
- The use of different electoral systems for different tiers of government means that votes remain of unequal value and the continued use of FPTP for Westminster elections produces unrepresentative results.

Overall the picture appears to be less one of a 'settlement' and far more one of a 'work in progress', with a programme of reform that has elevated the role and effectiveness of the judiciary and the House of Lords to create better checks on arbitrary government and yet has failed to tackle the decline in electoral turnout or re-establish public confidence in the political system.

This chapter assesses the impact of New Labour's constitutional reforms and looks at some criticisms of them.

The impact of New Labour's reforms: evolutionary or revolutionary?

The birth of New Labour is synonymous with the prospect of major constitutional renewal in Britain. One must not forget the context of New Labour's first appearance on the political scene — amid the sleaze and perceived moral bankruptcy of the final years of the Major government. It was a time when, according to the Labour Party manifesto of 1997, there seemed to be 'a national crisis of confidence in our political system'.

Labour's pledges were certainly 'revolutionary' in scope but to what extent did the areas most altered by the changes experience a renewal on a truly revolutionary scale? And to what extent did these changes collectively result in a 'constitutional settlement'?

- For many, the areas left unfinished or untouched, coupled with the lack of a single codified, formal document clearly defining the nature of the constitutional arrangements, undermine any claim that a 'settlement' has been achieved.
- For others, the evolutionary nature of the constitution itself means that any settlement will necessarily build on the cumulative nature of all previous constitutional alterations. On this basis, the desire for a 'final document' or 'settlement' is misleading since the UK constitution draws on conventions, precedents and prerogatives accumulated over several centuries.

Institutional renewal: evolution or revolution?

Parliament

As far as devolution, the passage of the Human Rights Act and the principle of parliamentary sovereignty are concerned, although the supremacy of Parliament has been preserved (for example, the Scotland Act 1998 asserts the Westminster Parliament's right to legislate in Scotland), the reality is that Parliament will never exercise its legislative right to terminate

The UK Supreme Court was created by the Constitutional Reform Act (2005)

regional assemblies. And although the courts cannot actually strike offending legislation down if it contravenes civil liberties contained in the Human Rights Act, the reality is that Parliament will do its utmost to ensure that legislation complies with the Act. In this respect there has been a significant, one might say 'revolutionary', shift in the status of the Westminster Parliament.

However, the Institute for Public Policy Research, in a publication entitled *Will New Labour Leave a Lasting Legacy?* (July 2010), cuts to the heart of the matter:

> In 1997 deference was still deeply embodied in our political system, most symbolically in the continued presence of hereditary peers in the House of Lords. An early success of the new administration was to abolish hereditary peers, but it never had the courage to go the whole way and move to an elected chamber — despite the promises of four manifestos.

The fact that New Labour failed to solve the 'retain, reform, replace, remove' debate over the future of the House of Lords should not necessarily undermine the significance of the 1999 Act and the confidence that it gave to the second chamber. Following the removal of all but 92 hereditary peers the Lords presented a far more effective and authoritative check on the party-orientated and heavily disciplined House of Commons. The greater legitimacy and professionalism of the Lords and the resulting rebalance in the relationship between the executive and Parliament as a consequence have contrived to stall further, definitive reforms of a parliamentary system that is functioning more effectively than it has done for generations.

The judiciary

If the reforming focus of New Labour's first term fell on the Lords, it was in the second term that attention turned to the role of the judiciary and its position within the branches of government. The two main goals of second term reforms to the judicial branch were to:

- separate the highest court of appeal in the land from the legislative branch of government
- restructure the roles and functions of the position of Lord Chancellor

In this area as in others, there were serious misgivings over whether a coherent plan of reform had been mapped out in advance. For example, the prospect of staunch resistance in the House of Lords to the complete abolition of the centuries-old post of Lord Chancellor resulted in a series of compromises and concessions:

- The Lord Chancellor's office would not be abolished but would remain to head up a new Department of Constitutional Affairs — still able to 'interfere' with the judicial branch, some argued.
- Early hopes that the new UK Supreme Court would have powers similar to its formidable US namesake were dashed. It became clear that the British version would, of course, not be able to declare parliamentary measures unconstitutional since there is no codified constitution to judge the constitutionality of legislation against.
- The exiting of existing Law Lords from Parliament was put on hold. The role of the Law Lords in enhancing legislation in the second chamber was considered to be too valuable to dispense with immediately. Instead, the Law Lords were to remain as members of both branches of government but would not be replaced when they retired.

The Constitutional Reform Act (2005) was responsible for the creation of both the Supreme Court and the Judicial Appointments Commission — the independent body that was to fill court vacancies when they arose. Although there has been a significant rise in the public profile of the court and a strong feeling that it stands impressively independent from the political system, tussles and uncertainties of independence or spheres of jurisdiction still occur (see Box 4.1). These serve to reflect the fact that New Labour's radical reforms — to complete the separation of judicial from legislative and executive powers — have not provided the 'settlement' that was expected.

Box 4.1

Funding: the threat to the independence of the Supreme Court

Lord Phillips, president of the new UK Supreme Court, maintained in February 2011 that the 'ad hoc' way the court is funded is a major threat to its independence. Lord Phillips stated that the fact that the court was required each year to persuade the ministry to hand over an operating budget 'by way of contribution' was 'not a satisfactory situation'.

He also claimed that there was a strong feeling that the Ministry of Justice saw the court as 'an outlying part of its empire'. Lord Phillips emphasised that members of the court should owe their primary loyalty to the president of the court and not the minister. He said that members of the ministry did not seem to appreciate this or comprehend the threat to the court's independence that this lack of clarity posed.

Table 4.1 Parliament and the judiciary

Area	Successes	Limitations
Parliament	• The removal of all but 92 hereditary peers under the 1999 Lords Reform Act • Specific reforms to some working practices of the House of Commons	• A stalling of the process of Lords reform: failure to agree on a way to move forward from the transitional House created in 1999 • No concerted effort to rebalance the relationship between the executive and the Commons
Judiciary	• The creation of an 'independent' Supreme Court in 2009 • An independent Judicial Appointments Commission to appoint judges • Extensive changes to the role and position of the Lord Chancellor	• Initial reforms for the role of Lord Chancellor were watered down • The Supreme Court's limited powers over parliamentary legislation disappointed liberal reformers

Rights and citizenship: evolution or revolution?

The passing of the Human Rights Act in 1998 which incorporated the European Convention on Human Rights into British domestic law finally put the rights of British citizens on a similar statutory footing to most other European states.

Yet in the wake of the increased terrorist threat following 9/11 and the London bombings in July 2005, the Human Rights Act seemed to become a thorn in the side of the administration that had championed it. For not only did British citizens possess rights, so too did prisoners, asylum seekers and terrorist suspects.

Odd, sometimes inexplicable, rulings that attempted to apply the Human Rights Act — ruling in favour of hijackers or terrorist suspects — in a variety of complex circumstances prompted the then Labour home secretary, John Reid, to claim that judges 'just don't get it'. In response, Conservative Party leader David Cameron maintained in 2006 that a Tory government would take the issue of rights seriously by pledging to 'reform, replace or scrap' an Act that was said to be responsible for hampering Britain's security services and, Cameron claimed, creating a culture of 'rights without responsibility' when what was really needed was a 'proper British Bill of Rights'.

Box 4.2

Cameron on the replacement of the Human Rights Act with a British Bill of Rights

'A modern British Bill of Rights needs to define the core values which give us our identity as a free nation [and be] a clear articulation of citizens' rights that British people can use in British courts.'

A British Bill of Rights 'would spell out the fundamental duties and responsibilities of people living in this country and protect the rights laid out in the European convention on human rights in clearer and more precise terms'.

Source: speech made by David Cameron at the Centre for Policy Studies in London in June 2006

From 'rights culture' to 'universal police powers'?

There is no doubt that the Human Rights Act has empowered the courts to protect the rights of citizens against the encroachment of state power far more effectively than was previously the case. Yet conversely, alongside this and the much vaunted Freedom of Information Act (see Chapter 2), came the suspension of habeas corpus (the protection against illegal imprisonment), the restriction of trial by jury and the assertion of the right of the state to remove an individual's citizenship. In addition, further moves to restrict rights and curtail freedoms include:

- The Regulation of Investigatory Powers Act in 2000 allowed government officials to invoke 'terror laws' to monitor individuals, often on spurious grounds (see Box 4.3).
- The Civil Contingencies Act of 2004 gave the government significant new powers in the event of an 'emergency' (see Box 4.4).
- Anti-social behaviour orders (ASBOs) became a prominent weapon in the state's armoury. Over 4,000 were issued in their first 5 years of existence and only a handful of applications were rejected. ASBOs became widely ridiculed when peculiar cases — such as the woman forbidden to wear a bikini in her garden — gained public notoriety.
- The Identity Card Bill was put before Parliament in 2004 and argued by the government to be an essential element of the campaign against terror. The debate over ID cards re-emerged fitfully for the next few years before finally being shelved.

Box 4.3

The abuse of 'terror laws', August 2010

One case that reached national prominence was that of Poole Borough Council which was accused of spying unfairly on a family. The council invoked powers under the Regulation of Investigatory Powers Act (RIPA) to establish whether the family lived at the address that they claimed to live at in order to fall into a more favourable school catchment area.

The council was found to have spied on the family on 21 separate occasions when taken before the Investigatory Powers Tribunal by the family in question. The tribunal found in favour of the family, stating that it was not a proper use of surveillance powers and acknowledged that RIPA laws were being abused or misused in numerous different ways.

Box 4.4

Perspectives on the Civil Contingencies Act, January 2004

- The *Guardian* declared that the Civil Contingencies Act was 'potentially the greatest threat to civil liberty that any Parliament is ever likely to consider'.
- The radical journal *Statewatch* went further: 'the powers available to the government and state agencies would be truly draconian...This is Britain's Patriot Act. At a stroke democracy could be replaced by totalitarianism'.

Source: *The Changing Constitution* by K. Harrison and T. Boyd (2006)

Needless to say, any conclusions based on New Labour's constitutional reforms in the area of rights present a confused picture. Such uncertainty is aptly summed up by the Human Rights Act itself — the passage of which was one of the most notable successes of the New Labour era. Reflecting on it, *The Economist* reported in 2004 that it was neither as feeble nor as drastic as its defenders and attackers have made out: 'The Human Rights Act has neither enabled more cases to be brought, nor made them much easier to win, since judges are still obliged to weigh individual rights against the common good.'

Table 4.2 Rights under New Labour

Area	Successes	Limitations
Rights	• The Human Rights Act of 1998 incorporated the European Convention on Human Rights into British domestic law • The Freedom of Information Act allowed far greater access to information held by government agencies and public bodies	• No British Bill of Rights proposed or introduced

Democratic renewal: how settled is the relationship between central, regional and local government?

The process of decentralisation was a key theme of Labour Party policy well before the arrival on the political scene of either Blair or Brown. And in many respects, devolution — the concept that had roots in party culture for generations — represented New Labour's principal success. The Institute for Public Policy Research in a publication entitled *Will New Labour Leave a Lasting Legacy?* (July 2010) concluded that: 'Without doubt, New Labour's most significant reform was the shift of power to Scotland, Wales and Northern Ireland. Devolution in the first instance saved the Union — appeasing Scotland, which had been threatening to break away for years.'

Regional devolution

There is no doubt that devolution has resulted in new relationships between the constituent parts of the UK and that the individual nations which comprise the UK are recognised more appropriately. In addition, the UK's heavily centralised state, prior to the process of devolution, has been replaced, some say, by a **quasi-federal** state which has allowed Britain to tread a middle ground between a parliamentary system and one characterised by **multi-level governance**.

With devolution came alternative electoral systems — some of them highly proportional in nature. And with these new electoral systems came new ways of governing. Coalitions became the 'norm' — Labour found itself working with Plaid Cymru in Wales and the Liberal Democrats in Scotland. Policies and legislation outside England's borders came to take on an appropriately consensual feel and flavour.

However, a key question posed by devolution is whether a process of asymmetric devolution can provide any real long-term stability for the UK since in Vernon Bogdanor's words: 'Asymmetrical devolution breaches the principle of equal rights for all citizens of the UK. Those in non-English parts of the UK enjoy devolution, while the English don't.'

If several others factors are added to the equation, such as:
- Scotland still receiving 20% more per head in public spending than is the case in England
- Wales being over-represented at Westminster, returning 40 MPs when a comparable population in England would return 33
- Scotland, Wales and Northern Ireland retaining (albeit part-time) secretaries of state at cabinet level while England does not
  then the imbalance appears not merely awkward but also undemocratic.

The Conservative Party has long predicted that devolution would eventually result in the breakup of the UK and yet its stance has modified considerably in recent years. From William Hague urging Conservatives to participate fully in the first regional elections in 1999 to David Cameron paving the way for a Welsh referendum on legislative powers, the party's embrace of devolved government has been rapid.

But critics of the process argue that the constitutional position of the UK is now less stable that it was. The Acts to bring in devolution will not help to clarify the relationship between the nations should nationalist parties push for further independence.

The developments have therefore raised profound constitutional questions over the future of the UK:
- The potential for tension or conflict is perceived as being very real and the absence of a formally written constitution could prove costly in this area.
- Questions over the effectiveness of a constitutionally 'balanced' federal UK, where one nation is overwhelmingly more populous and better resourced than all the others, remain of concern.
- A lack of clarity on the basis of citizenship and access to welfare rights — with the 'special need' of Scotland in the areas of education and health — appears at odds with principles of equality and rights.

Others point to the long-term survival of the UK's evolutionary constitution and its ability to ride out far greater crises (most notably the secession of the Irish Republic) than any that devolution could present.

Box 4.5

Does devolution signal an end to the 'United' Kingdom?

Yes

- Serious constitutional problems, such as unequal representation between the regions at Westminster and the unanswered West Lothian question, have undermined confidence in the constitutional framework of the UK.
- The lack of an effective solution to English regional representation has resulted in disquiet in England over the inequality of the process of devolution.
- Policy divergence over basic rights — to education, healthcare and welfare — has undermined any sense of a common basis for rights in the UK.
- Confusion over accountability, greater bureaucracy and increased costs will mean that demands for a full breakup of the UK will grow.
- Referendums in Wales over primary legislative powers and proposed independence referendums by the SNP in Scotland make the process of further separation and breakup seem inevitable.

No

- Polls suggest that a feeling of Britishness remains as strong as it did before devolution and only small minorities in the regions favour full independence.
- The greater autonomy enjoyed by the nations has calmed the momentum for full independence that might otherwise have proved irresistible and has enabled people to feel that their government is more responsive.
- Those doubting the ability of the regional governments to stand up to political tests, such as minority government rule, have been proved wrong.
- Policy divergence merely reflects different priorities in different regions.
- The resolution of years of unrest in Northern Ireland has been a particularly notable achievement.

Local government

But undermining New Labour's claim to have provided a true 'settlement' to central/regional/local relations was its reluctance to truly 'renew' local democracy. Critics point to the timidity of New Labour's plans to reinvigorate local government, even at the outset in 1997. Democratic renewal at a local level seemed to hinge on the arrival of locally elected mayors and on a better deal for citizens by the capping of council tax rises.

Some impressive reforms were suggested, primarily by the Lyons Inquiry which produced several reports between 2004 and 2007 concerning local government finance, but many never saw the light of day. Instead, alongside New Labour's reluctance to devolve government power to a local level came progressively more disappointing voter turnout at local elections, revealing the electorate's growing disillusionment with the brand of local democracy on offer.

Box 4.6

The Lyons Report: Reinvigorating Local Government

Sir Michael Lyons: 'I believe that local government is an essential part of our system of government today. Local government's place-shaping role — using powers and influence creatively to promote the wellbeing of a community and its citizens — is crucial to help improve satisfaction and prosperity through greater local choice and flexibility.'

A key recommendation was for greater flexibility for local authorities with less control from the centre; new powers to levy a supplementary business rate and a new power to charge for domestic waste to help manage pressures on council tax, and an end to capping of council tax. Despite widespread support, few significant recommendations had been taken up.

Source: adapted from *The Lyons Inquiry into Local Government* (2007 Report)

Table 4.3 Devolution under New Labour

Area	Successes	Limitations
Decentralisation	• The creation of Greater London Authority and a London mayor • Further elected mayors introduced in other cities	• A failure to resolve the role and significance of local government • Just 12 local authorities adopted elected mayors
Devolution	• The creation of three regional governments: two — Scotland and Northern Ireland — had primary legislative powers; one — Wales — had secondary legislative powers	• Criticisms that services were uneven • Proposals for English regional devolution ended by North-Eastern 'no' vote in 2004 referendum

Ultimately, Labour's attempts to reinvigorate local democracy appear to be as confused as the messages that it received from the public. On one day the government might be reprimanded for 'over-regulation', for its targets, its edicts and its heavy-handed intervention if services were considered to be below par. On another day, calls for repressive government action to end 'post code lotteries' (the wild fluctuations in levels of service depending on where citizens lived) might abound. Again, the lack of a clear philosophy on the direction of the central/local relationship is evident, as Toynbee and Walker (2010) conclude: 'The public remained ambiguous about local democracy… It would have helped if Labour had overarching principles on the duty of the state to intervene and interfere and on the boundary of individual liberty and personal risk.'

Elections and referendums: evolution or revolution?

When New Labour swept to power in 1997 it did so after securing 43% of the votes from a 71% turnout: two-thirds of the parliamentary seats were scooped up with less than a third of the support of the electorate. In 2001, an equally emphatic parliamentary majority enjoyed positive support from less than a quarter of the electorate. By 2005, that support had fallen to just over a fifth. Toynbee and Walker (2010) maintain that: 'a far bigger scandal than expenses was the lack of popular support for the all-powerful governments that whipped MPs through the lobbies'.

Ensuring that representative assemblies were made up in proportion to votes cast was a principle not lost on New Labour. Its 1997 manifesto boldly stated that: 'We are committed to a referendum on the voting system for the House of Commons. An independent Commission on voting systems will be appointed early to recommend a proportional alternative to FPTP.'

Regional assemblies, the Greater London Assembly and the proposed plans for the English regions were all built on far fairer voting systems than the one used for the Westminster Parliament. Indeed, New Labour's drive for greater representation appeared to have overtaken even the people that it was intended to empower. The referendums that legitimised the London mayor and the assemblies of both London and Wales (see Table 2.2 in Chapter 2) were hardly emphatic endorsements of these new tiers of government and the system of English regional governments that John Prescott had toiled over for several years fell at the first hurdle when the people of the North East voted against it in 2004.

First-past-the-post remains

Yet Blair and Brown both failed to fully support the one reform that would have ensured that a government could never again secure twice as many seats as its opposition — on the back of just 3 percentage points more votes (as New Labour did in 2005). While Blair shelved the suggestion of AV+ which emerged from the Jenkins enquiry that he himself commissioned in 1997, Brown failed to provide adequate parliamentary time for his own 2009 announcement in support of the alternative vote.

The problem of non-participation was identified by New Labour, worried over but never solved. The age bar to standing as a candidate was lowered to 18, postal voting (with its associated rise in electoral fraud) was made far more accessible and the creation of an independent Electoral Commission made inroads into greater transparency of party funding. Yet, in spite of all the rhetoric concerning participation and representation, the Labour Party left office in 2010 with an unrepresentative voting system for the House of Commons still firmly in place.

| Table 4.4 | Summary of reforms in the area of democracy and participation |

Area	Successes	Limitations
Elections	• Alternative electoral systems used for elections to the European Parliament, to regional assemblies and for the London mayor	• Failure to implement the reforms suggested by the Jenkins Report for elections to Westminster • Failure to deliver on a 2009 pledge to adopt the alternative vote
Referendums	• Referendums used prior to the creation of devolved assemblies and for the London mayor	• Pledged referendums on entry to the European single currency and on electoral reform never materialised. • Referendum on EU constitution was dropped

From left to right: how have the New Labour reforms been criticised?

The Conservative perspective

'Conservatism' and the arrangements of the British constitution have long been seen as enjoying a particularly close fit. The traditional Conservative focus on strong government and gradual, 'evolutionary' change, set alongside a carefully managed balance between the authority of the state and the liberty of the individual has, supporters maintain, provided centuries of stability and prosperity.

Conservatism and constitutional change

When change has been needed, Conservatives have recognised and supported it (see Box 4.7). But they have also strived to protect and preserve key institutions of state from threat or interference from abroad and to maintain underpinning constitutional principles and practices — such as parliamentary sovereignty, and the majoritarian electoral system — from change.

Box 4.7

Examples of Conservative support for constitutional change

- 1958   The Life Peerages Act reinvigorated the legislative role of the House of Lords.
- 1972   A Conservative government under Edward Heath signed up to the Treaty of Rome which took the UK into the European Union.
- 1979   Significant reform to the scrutinising functioning of select committees in the House of Commons was one of Margaret Thatcher's first acts.

Under Margaret Thatcher a growing dislocation emerged between traditional Conservative constitutional values which sought to resist further European integration and to preserve the integrity of governmental authority (by opposing growing pressure for devolved government) and policy decisions on a practical level which saw the UK signing up to the Single European Act and a greater willingness to seek settlement in Northern Ireland by engaging with republican groups. As previously discussed (see Chapter 1), the 1980s were also a period of intense constitutional strain as the informal, unofficial arrangements that oversaw the delicate balance of power between central and local government were eroded.

Conservatism and New Labour's constitutional settlement

The far-reaching, relatively successful and widely-supported programme of constitutional change undertaken by the Labour Party from 1997 shook the Conservative Party to its core and was a contributory factor in the party losing its direction for the best part of a decade. Philip Lynch in an article on Conservatism and constitutional reform (2008) writes: 'Labour's reforms created a dilemma for the Conservatives: how should a party committed to the status quo respond when much of it has been swept away?'

A reactionary response to the process of devolution, with each transferral of power having been legitimised by popular referendum, would have been as inappropriate as a staunch defence of the hereditary principle of the traditional House of Lords. Instead the Conservative Party took some time to find its voice on constitutional matters, but progressively highlighted what it perceived to be the damage that New Labour's incoherent and piecemeal reforms had had on the overall functioning of the state. The Conservatives focused on:

- the uneven process of devolution which had resulted in different tiers of government with different levels of power
- the growth in the power of the judiciary following the passage of the Human Rights Act
- the erosion of the principle of parliamentary sovereignty through further European integration

The Conservative Party has challenged the notion that the New Labour reforms have resulted in anything resembling a coherent 'settlement' to the constitutional arrangements of the UK. Under David Cameron, the Party's Democracy Task Force, chaired by Kenneth Clark, pointed squarely at Blair's style of leadership in 2007 as the group's first report *An End to Sofa Government* reaffirmed the significance of collective cabinet decision-making and proposed the strengthening of the Ministerial Code. A further report in 2009, *Power to the People: Rebuilding Parliament*, pushed for reforms to the House of Commons to make its ability to hold the executive to account more effective.

Radical Conservatism

More radical Conservative perspectives on New Labour's constitutional settlement urge a far more dramatic response to the 'damage' that has been done to the constitution's defining features. Three areas of particular focus are:

- the undermining of parliamentary sovereignty by human rights legislation
- the undermining of the unitary state — with its government at the centre in Westminster — by the process of devolution
- the undermining of Britain's organic common law system by excessive European integration and the primacy of EU law

However, in 2011, prevaricating between proposals for reaffirming key constitutional principles and more radical suggestions to overturn rights legislation or withdraw from the European Union, the Conservative Party found itself in a similar position to the party that it had replaced — without a coherent vision of Britain's constitutional future. Whether by evolutionary steps or radical reform, the Conservatives will need to establish a framework to achieve their own 'constitutional settlement'. Further discussion of the coalition government's constitutional direction appears in Chapter 6.

The liberal perspective

There is no doubt that the Labour Party adopted many proposals that were being advanced by those seeking a liberal constitutional settlement. The Human Rights Act, a Freedom of Information Act, regional government and a reformed House of Lords would all have featured at the top of any wish-list compiled by liberal reformers. Indeed, many on the left would conclude that the Labour Party has made the UK a fairer, more transparent and more participative state than ever before.

The evidence of the close working relationship between the Liberal Democrat and Labour parties in the 1990s is clear and the partnership shaped many proposals that would become the principle features of Labour's constitutional reform programme.

However, the reforms that the Labour Party advanced would steadily disappoint liberal reformers. Some criticised the timidity of the reforms. For others, it was their piecemeal delivery which meant that any clear vision — or a sustained constitutional 'movement' — failed to materialise.

New Labour and the liberal agenda: citizenship

The expansion of rights and liberties that occurred during the period of New Labour government ensured that the party left a Britain that was far more tolerant than the Britain that it inherited. However, the raft of policies to limit freedom has prompted critics on the liberal-left of the political spectrum to conclude that existing tensions between policies to empower citizens and policies to deter are starker and more confusing than ever before.

Conclusion

New Labour's radical yet incoherent constitutional reforms are perhaps best exemplified in the area of rights. The media pilloried New Labour for its seeming obsession with rights — the logical conclusion of which, they said, was the fostering of a 'culture of entitlement' within society. However, the simultaneous growth of state regulation and anti-terror legislation is argued to have extended the state's reach and infringed rights further than ever before.

New Labour's reforms were certainly revolutionary in the way that they reorganised the relationships between the institutions of state, created new levels of representation and enhanced opportunities for participation. However, any notion that there has been a constitutional settlement in any coherent sense is belied by areas of unfinished business and, ultimately, by the lack of any clear constitutional goal from the outset. The final words of Anthony King's authoritative text *The British Constitution* reveal that: 'the new British Constitution thus remains a mess. It is probably, on balance, a benign mess, one that people can live with, as well as being a novel and thought-provoking mess. But it is a mess all the same.'

Task 4.1

1 Construct a chart to identify and evaluate the effectiveness of reforms limiting the power of the executive between 1997 and 2010.

Guidance

1 Use a piece of A4 paper to construct a chart similar to the one below under the heading 'Limiting the power of the executive branch 1997–2010'. Much information for this task can be found in the first four chapters of the book but particularly in the discussion on the 'evolutionary or revolutionary' reforms under New Labour governments. Start by thinking about rights legislation, reforms to the legislative and judicial branches (especially the Lords) and the powers that have been devolved to the regions.

	Reform	Effectiveness
1		
2		
3		
4		
5		

Task 4.2

Read the extract below and answer the questions which follow.

Figures published by the Liberal Democrats show that local councils carried out 20,000 covert operations using RIPA [Regulation of Investigatory Powers Act] laws. These operations represent a gross misuse of terror laws and a mass invasion of privacy which cannot be justified by subsequent actions — fewer than 10% of them resulted in prosecution, caution or fixed penalty notices. Julia Goldsworthy MP said, 'The government has seen civil liberties as little more than a temporary inconvenience. Slowly but surely freedoms have been eroded.'

The loss of liberty is one of the big legacies of an appalling, shallow, dishonest and vindictive government, which has failed the hopes and trust of so many. None of the brilliant lawyers and academics who leap to the defence of the Human Rights Act can deny that the government's and Home Office's contempt for rights are habitual, and appear to be an ineradicable part of their nature that the HRA cannot restrain.

There are scores and scores of examples where the HRA can be shown to be utterly useless in the face of state power and where it is ignored by police, government agencies and local authorities. Neither the HRA or these plans to 'improve' rights legislation will do anything to protect us from a government whose default position is to attack our freedoms and undermine our democracy.

This is the simple reality of the situation, which the HRA defenders seem unable or unwilling to grasp.

Source: adapted from 'The Human Rights Act can't restrain the government' by Henry Porter, the novelist and political commentator, *Guardian*, March 2009

1 What evidence is there for suggesting that the Human Rights Act is ineffective?
2 How would you mount a defence of the Human Rights Act?

Guidance

1 Look back at the sections covering the Human Rights Act and contrast this to the sentiments of Henry Porter, especially in the final paragraphs of the source. What does the Act do? How does Henry Porter criticise the Act?
2 Think about how the Human Rights Act has enshrined basic freedoms and checked the power of the executive. Think of some specific examples of when the Act has been used to provide a check on executive power.

Task 4.3

1   Visit the website of the Committee on Standards in Public Life: **www.public-standards. gov.uk**. The committee refers to itself as 'an independent advisory body to the government' set up 'to deal with concerns about unethical conduct amongst MPs, including accepting financial incentives for tabling Parliamentary questions, and issues over procedures for appointment to public bodies'.

● Click on 'Our Work' across the top.

● Click on 'Annual Reports' on the left-hand side.

● Scan down the reports and click on one of the most recent Annual Reports to download or open it.

2   Write a short summary of the material contained within one of the reports on the Committee on Standards in Public Life website. Explain briefly what the report relates to in constitutional terms. Try to set it within the wider context of the UK's uncodified constitutional arrangements.

3   To what extent does the work of the Committee on Standards in Public Life provide evidence for those arguing that the UK is acquiring a constitution 'by the back door'?

Guidance

3   Refer back to the section on the growing level of constitutional codification in the UK, towards the end of Chapter 1. Is there evidence for this? A large number of Acts of constitutional significance have been passed since 1997 — can you make a list of them? In what ways have they 'codified' the UK's arrangements? Good examples are those that relate to the House of Lords and to devolution but there are many more.

Further reading

● Harker, L. and Oppenheim, C. (2010) *Will New Labour Leave a Lasting Legacy?* Institute for Public Policy Research.

● Lynch, P. (2008) 'Conservatism and constitutional reform', *Politics Review*, Vol. 18, No.4.

● Toynbee, P. and Walker, D. (2010) *The Verdict: Did Labour Change Britain?* Granta.

● Democracy Task Force publication, *Power to the People: Rebuilding Parliament*: www.conservatives.com/pdf/dtfpaper.pdf

● UK Supreme Court: www.supremecourt.gov.uk — click on FAQs

● Unlock Democracy website (for an insight into one of the leading advocates of the liberal agenda): www.unlockdemocracy.org.uk

A codified constitution for the UK: yes or no?

A century after the UK's constitutional arrangements were shaken to their core as limits were placed on the historic power of the Lords and the suffragettes campaigned for equal voting rights, constitutional reform rose to the top of the political agenda once more in the second decade of the twenty-first century.

The expenses scandal, the electoral legitimacy of a coalition government, the setting aside of basic human rights in response to an increased terror threat and the perceived lack of accountability of MPs themselves all placed the uncodified nature of a constitution that sustained such arrangements under the spotlight.

As has been discussed, Britain does have a written constitution — it is just that it sprawls across innumerable works of reference, statutes and laws. What Britain doesn't have, as confirmed by Colin Pilkington in the *Politics Today Companion to the British Constitution*, is 'a short single-volume constitution that has been neatly collated and formally codified for easy reference, infallible accuracy and binding force'.

Quite why Britain even exists without a formal codified structure is an important question. Furthermore, the opinion of Charter 88, the pressure group campaigning for codification — that 'unwritten rules are dangerous' — fuels debate over the direction that the British state has taken in recent decades as a direct consequence of its uncodified framework.

Why doesn't the UK have a codified constitution?

While the arguments for the codification of the UK's constitutional arrangements have gathered pace over recent decades, so too has the actual process of codification. There may not be any real coherence to the process, and the main principle of codification — that of creating a single, definitive document — may not be the ultimate goal, but the UK's constitutional arrangements appear to be taking on a distinctly codified character. Three examples are:

- the relationship between the centre and the regions which is clearly set out in the devolution Acts, codifying the powers of the Scottish Parliament and the Welsh Assembly
- Britain's relationship with Europe which is codified in the various treaties that have been signed, including the most recent Lisbon Treaty
- rules and regulations governing the conduct of elections which are overseen by the Electoral Commission and the operation of political parties which have been codified in the form of the Political Parties, Elections and Referendums Act

---

Box 5.1

Codification: the last taboo?

By the turn of the last century a reforming government [had] altered many constitutional rules and added to the statute-base of the British constitution. The apparent taboo which had seemed to prevent British Governments from making planned changes to the constitution was broken.

Source: R. Brazier, *Constitutional Reform* (2008)

However, in spite of pronouncements in favour of codification coming as recently as 2008 — when Jack Straw's work on a new British Bill of Rights and Responsibilities could, he claimed, have been the first step along the road to codification — Britain remains one of only a handful of modern democratic states without a single codified document.

Stability and reform

Many commentators put the lack of codification down to the UK's intrinsic stability. Nigel Morris, home affairs correspondent for the *Independent*, contrasts the UK's steadiness with 'the governing elites of many European nations, such as France and Germany…who have been forced to draw up constitutions in response to popular revolt or war'. The UK, remarkably free from the kind of revolutionary fever that swept the continent throughout the nineteenth century, has never experienced a single, definitive moment in which the rewriting of the rules and regulations which govern the state would have been deemed appropriate.

As a result, the constitutional arrangements of the UK have developed in an 'ad hoc' fashion, blending common law, case law, legislation emanating from

Europe, parliamentary statutes and important historical documents: the whole — again according to Jack Straw — 'existing in hearts and minds and habits as much as it does in law'.

Box 5.2

Why doesn't the UK have a written constitution, and does it matter?

'If it ain't broke, don't fix it,' argue opponents of a written constitution, who insist that the existing arrangements, however piecemeal their development, have worked well in practice. There are, moreover, formidable practical problems to be overcome before such a document can be drawn up. Would it be wide-ranging and largely abstract or would it list individuals' rights in detail and provide an exhaustive summary of Britain's constitutional settlement? If the latter, it could prove beyond the grasp of most of the citizens it would be designed to protect.

Source: extract from 'Why doesn't the UK have a written constitution, and does it matter?' by Nigel Morris, *Independent*, February 2008

© The Independent

Key constitutional landmarks

The barons who forced King John to sign the Magna Carta in 1215 would clearly never have imagined that their demands would inspire constitutional principles all over the globe for the best part of a millennium. What started as a drive to protect the interests of wealthy landowners against arbitrary rule ended up enshrining fundamental principles, such as the right to a fair trial and protection from unlawful imprisonment.

Further landmarks that have influenced Britain's constitution and have contributed to its evolutionary nature are to be found in the Bill of Rights of 1689, which asserted key parliamentary rights, and the Great Reform Act of 1832, which extended the franchise and set Britain on the path to universal suffrage. More recently, EU membership and the Human Rights Act are further examples of fundamental constitutional principles that have been added to arrangements in what is sometimes described as a 'haphazard fashion'.

But how useful are these historical documents or the body of principles that together they make up? The original Charter 88 argued that the constitutional arrangements, as they stood back in 1988, demonstrated 'how vulnerable Britain has always been to elective dictatorship. The consequence is that today the British have fewer legal rights and less democracy than many other West Europeans.'

Needless to say, assertions that key institutions of the British state were in dire need of constitutional protection have proved to be more than founded amid expenses scandals, the marginalisation of Parliament, exhaustive inquiries into the legality of executive decisions and the infringement of basic rights.

The impetus for constitutional change

The last few decades have provided countless examples of constitutions being ripped up, revamped or revised. The Second World War, the collapse of the fascist dictatorships of Spain and Portugal in the 1970s, the ending of Soviet control of Eastern Europe in the 1980s and 1990s all resulted in the proliferation of new binding documents concerning the framework of states. It is estimated that two-thirds of the constitutions in operation today have been written since the Second World War. The oldest codified document in Europe is Swiss, enacted in 1874.

For the UK, as well as for other states, the feeling that there is a need to revamp the constitutional arrangements has grown steadily — each episode of political mismanagement or decision making based on questionable legitimacy giving rise to further calls for codification. There is also a sense that the arrangements which govern the state — the distribution of power and the locations of authority within it — are out of step with the stated principles and characteristics as determined by the constitution. In Andrew Heywood's words, in *Politics* (1997):

> In general, it can be said that political conflicts assume a constitutional dimension only when those demanding change seek to redraw and not merely re-adjust, the rules of the political game. Constitutional change is therefore about the re-apportionment of both power and political authority.

Has the lack of a codified constitution allowed the UK state to become 'hollowed out'?

For some commentators, the functioning of the British government has changed so radically since the 1980s that any notion of the constitutional arrangements remaining based on traditional understandings is both misconceived and out of date. In fact, many constitutional principles —such as 'parliamentary sovereignty' and the 'unitary state'— are, in any practical sense, obsolete.

A casual look at the branches of government and the institutions of the British state might lead one to conclude that in both form and substance the 'government' of the UK is remarkably similar to one that might have existed for several centuries. In reality, the state, some say, has been 'hollowed out' (see Box 5.3) and consequently any debate on the merit of recent constitutional reforms or transformations misses the point.

The *real* transformation of state power has not been conducted by Acts of Parliament; set out in manifestos or legitimised by referendums. The key areas of change have not been neatly contained within a more-or-less coherent package of constitutional reform. Instead, a 'quiet revolution' has occurred that, to some, has turned the nature of state power in Britain on its head.

Box 5.3

Key term: the 'hollowed-out state'

The 'hollowing out' of the state refers to the steady dispersal of political power to localities, independent organisations and supranational bodies (like the European Union). The way that the economy is managed, that welfare is provided and that public services are controlled is wholly different in today's modern state to the way that political decisions were made in the past — by formal political structures and according to traditional constitutional principles.

Several factors — that stretch from the day-to-day operation of the British government to the process of globalisation — underpin this theory:

- The **transformation of decision making** at the heart of British government since the 1980s has been significant. The restructuring of the traditional role of the civil service and the creation of semi-autonomous government 'agencies' — for instance, the DVLA or 'Jobcentre Plus' — has blurred the lines of responsibility and accountability (see Box 5.4). The rise of influential but unaccountable special advisors, quangos and think tanks with a direct input into government policy has steadily transferred power from the conventional locations and rendered traditional structures of parliamentary scrutiny largely ineffective.
- The process of **privatisation** has meant that successive governments have not had the same level of control over Britain's economic base. In addition, the growth in multinational organisations has further weakened the capacity of any national government to influence the direction of its economy.

- The rise of an increasingly **regulatory state** has accompanied the dismantling of key state-run industries. The provision of services at central and local levels is now monitored and controlled by powerful but non-elected bodies with resulting questions over legitimacy and democracy.
- Membership of the **European Union** has seen political power steadily drain from Britain's national institutions. When combined with membership of other organisations, such as the United Nations and NATO, and with the devolution of power to the regions, the alteration in the nature of decision making in the UK has been profound.
- The process of **globalisation** has ensured that any state's policy decisions are not the product of national debate but instead of global forces. In the UK in particular, the gap between traditional understandings of the workings of government and the reality — which involves an intricate web of global institutions — is particularly marked.

Box 5.4

Accountability and the 'hollowed-out state'

How far is a minister responsible for the actions of an agency? This was a question raised in 1995 when the chief executive of the Prison Service, Derek Lewis, was made to resign after a number of prison escapes, while the then Home Secretary, Michael Howard, survived on the rather dubious grounds that this was not a policy matter but an organisational matter. A similar situation occurred in November 2004 when the head of the Child Support Agency, Doug Smith, resigned after investigation by the Work and Pensions Select Committee revealed a catalogue of failures in the Agency; the Secretary of State, Alan Johnson, remained in office.

Source: K. Harrison and T. Boyd, *The Changing Constitution* (2006)

So, the dispersal, or diffusion, of political power in the UK in recent decades has resulted in the growth of a far less accountable decision-making structure. The traditional constitutional principles of 'responsible' government no longer apply in an environment dominated by non-elected bodies which appear to be beyond traditional democratic checks. And with these shifts in the balance of power showing no signs of slowing, to many, the traditional constitutional arrangements of the UK have either disappeared or buckled under irresistible pressures. Calls for codification are almost impossible to ignore.

What are the arguments in favour of codifying the UK's constitution?

The calls for a radical review of the UK's constitutional arrangement are certainly compelling. There is a fundamental lack of clarity at the heart of the constitutional arrangements of the UK which has given rise to many difficult and controversial situations, each one an obvious consequence of a constitution characterised by ambiguous constitutional roles and principles.

Four key themes are identified as arguments in favour of codifying the existing arrangements.

Codification would provide clarity and be of educative value

One of the central arguments against the arrangements in the UK hinges on the lack of clarity at their core. The absence of a single authoritative document means that it is often conventions and traditions that provide guidelines to political action rather than clear-cut and easily consultable rights, rules and regulations. The argument that there is no popular desire for constitutional change is seen as being far more a reflection of the mystery and secrecy that surrounds the UK's arrangements than a true expression of the will of the people. Advocates of a codified document maintain that people *do* want to have their rights effectively protected and *do* want to see the existence of clear-cut checks placed on the powers of the executive.

Box 5.5

The problems associated with the UK's flexible constitution

Whereas in the past the flexibility of the British Constitution had been regarded as an asset, the basis of good government, from the 1970s there were increasing doubts about the effectiveness of some institutions. The political system seemed less successful in 'delivering the goods' than it had been.

Source: D. Watts, *British Government and Politics: a Comparative Guide* (2006)

In the USA, a single authoritative document which sets out the core values of the state and of the rights of citizens serves to bring together the values upon which the nation stands. The disparate nature of the UK's constitutional principles has the opposite effect — it hinders notions of citizenship and civic responsibility. In addition, the teaching of citizenship, rights and responsibilities in schools lacks a coherent educative core and the British state is the poorer for it.

Codification would provide a check on executive power

For liberal-leaning critics of the UK's arrangements, suspicions of the steady accumulation of state power appear to have been well founded. The erosion of the restraining features of the traditional constitution during the process of centralisation provided much ammunition for the supporters of codification. Without a codified constitution the relationships between the branches of government remain unclear; the relationship between the citizens and the state are open to change and as a consequence of the sovereignty of Parliament, no effective limits are placed on the government of the day.

In addition to this, the growth in government — with the seemingly indiscriminate rise in the power and influence of special advisors, quangos and other non-elected figures and groups who have a significant say in the political process — is a direct result of the confusion over the exact nature of the UK's constitutional arrangements.

Box 5.6

Unchecked executive power

The UK government has too much unchecked power, inherited from our feudal past. We need to catch up with the rest of the world by adopting a written constitution designed to limit what governments can do in our name. Too often, governments are free to casually compromise our fundamental rights and freedoms. We need stronger safeguards and to entrench the right to redress.

Source: **www.unlockdemocracy.org.uk**

Codification would see the effective entrenchment of rights

The Governance of Britain declared in 2007 that a 'Bill of Rights and Duties could give people a clear idea of what we can expect from public authorities and from each other, and a framework for giving practical effect to our common values'.

Rather like reform of the Lords, the initial adoption of the European Convention on Human Rights into British domestic law in the form of the Human Rights Act was to be just the first stage in the creation of a British Bill of Rights. But by the time the Human Rights Act came into force in 2000 — welcomed by Jack Straw as 'the first bill of rights this country has seen for three centuries' — it already seemed to be clear that the Labour Party's enthusiasm for its earlier commitment to the development of a full British Bill of Rights had waned.

Supporters of a British Bill of Rights maintain that the only way to effectively protect the rights of citizens from arbitrary change is to entrench them within a codified constitution. For instance, the Labour government was able to curtail basic rights — such as those contained within the Human Rights Act — by detaining terrorist suspects under anti-terror legislation. Such powers, with small modifications, have been maintained by the coalition government. Codification would make the rights of citizens far more difficult to curtail as special procedures would be needed to change them.

Codification would result in the modernisation of the UK's political arrangements

The ambiguity of having two entirely separate principles guiding constitutional arrangements — one theoretical (that of parliamentary sovereignty) and one practical (devolution and the transferring of legislative powers in certain areas to Europe) is unsustainable. Many commentators see the current arrangements as the product of a pre-democratic age and entirely out of keeping with modern day politics.

The UK's arrangements are also seen as being absurdly out of keeping with all other members of the European Union (EU) — the UK is the only member of the EU without a codified constitution. Put simply, the current arrangements are not normal and, for many, are to blame for Britain's steady economic decline as an electoral system that sees power swing from one party to another — each with sizeable majorities able to make rapid and wide-ranging changes.

In many ways, the process of complete codification would do little more than draw together all the disparate, but codified, arrangements which govern the UK at the moment.

What are the arguments against codifying the UK's constitution?

The central argument in favour of the UK's uncodified constitutional arrangements is that the constitution has evolved so successfully over such a long period of time. The body of rules and regulations that provides the framework for the effective functioning of the British state is not the product of a particular mood or point in time, nor is it left to unelected judges to determine what is and what is not 'constitutional'. Its shape and form lie in the hands of a regularly elected, highly responsive legislature and it exhibits an appropriate degree of flexibility to ensure that it can easily adapt to changing social, economic and political circumstances.

Under the current arrangements, the constitution 'works'

Supporters of the UK's constitution point to its *organic* nature — it has adapted over time, as and when the need for change has been proven. Any moves to change the existing arrangements would also challenge the prevailing political culture. Guiding principles, such as parliamentary sovereignty, and central characteristics of the UK, such as its unitary nature, would be swept away. The authority of the Westminster Parliament would be irreversibly undermined.

The lack of demand for codification is largely down to the fact that the current constitutional arrangements 'work'. Take for instance the steady erosion of monarchical power — this has enabled the country to retain the best features of its royal heritage while reshaping the working of the state without major disruption or turmoil.

Box 5.7

John Griffith on the British constitution (1986)

The Constitution is what happens.

Source: quoted in P. Hennessey, *Whitehall* (1989)

Under the current arrangements, checks and balances do exist

The fact that the UK's constitution is flexible is not to say that it is without significant checks. There are several examples of governments with substantial majorities being forced to compromise on legislation or policies, such as plans to elect police and crime commissioners (defeated in the Lords, May 2011) and Gurkha settlement plans (defeated in the Commons, April 2009). In addition, recent judgements in the courts, primarily based on the Human Rights Act, have found against governments and prompted extensive revision of laws.

All this suggests that there is a significant amount of 'balance' between the branches of government.

Codification would not result in enhanced democracy

The creation of a codified constitution would not necessarily enhance democracy since disputes over the relationships between the branches of government or between the citizen and the state would be resolved by unelected judges. In addition, these unelected judges would have the capacity to declare Acts of Parliament unconstitutional, thereby catapulting them into the political arena.

It is often argued that the delicate and complex arrangements that characterise the UK's constitution cannot be reduced to a brief document — any sense that the result would provide either clarity or an educative function is deeply mistaken. Any bid to reduce the way that the prime minister, cabinet, the wider government, Parliament and alternative centres of political power interact, to a short document would be doomed to failure.

Box 5.8

The power of unelected judges under a codified constitution: a controversy not confined to UK shores

The enactment of a Human Rights Charter would confer power on 'unelected judges' to make decisions which should be reserved to elected officials. These include decisions striking a balance between the human rights or freedoms of individuals and the claims of society to limit or qualify those rights or freedoms. In a statutory charter such decisions might affect the way in which Acts of Parliament are interpreted and applied and official powers exercised.

Source: *In Praise of Unelected Judges*, 2009 Report, the John Curtin Institute of Public Policy, Public Policy Forum, Perth, Australia

---

Codification is unachievable

The idea that the UK could even begin to work out a process for codifying its constitutional arrangements, let alone actually execute the task, seems almost impossible. In addition, the question over who would endorse or legitimise the end product remains highly questionable.

Box 5.9

Norton on the impossibility of codification (1998)

Under the existing constitution there is no body that can authorize or legitimise a new constitution. The one thing that Parliament cannot do is use its power under the doctrine of parliamentary sovereignty to destroy that doctrine, because its legitimacy to do so derives from the very power which it seeks to destroy. To create a new constitution, it would be necessary to start from scratch — which would cause constitutional and political turmoil that would not be worth enduring.

Source: quoted in Bentley et al., *British Politics in Focus* (2004)

The process by which the constitution would be constructed and ratified is clearly a serious obstacle to even beginning the process of reform. To suggest that Britain ought to fall into line with other European nations — nations that, many argue, lack links with their political past on the same level that the UK does — could be seen as being deeply mistaken.

Box 5.10

John Young on the 'specialness' of the UK's constitutional arrangements

British national identity is arguably stronger because the country has been able gradually to develop its unique, unwritten constitution. Both this strong national identity and the unwritten constitution make the participation in supranational institutions difficult: Continental states are more used to permanent involvements and to ornate, written constitutions.

Source: J. Young, *Britain and Europe: 1945–1992* (1993)

Conclusion

While the difficulties associated with full codification of the constitution cannot be underestimated, it is achievable. Supporters of the creation of a codified constitution are not persuaded by those who insist that Britain is unique in the modern world in its *inability* to codify its constitutional arrangements.

The process would not be an easy one — it would involve not merely intellectual choices but also political ones. There would be intense debate over what to include and what to leave out. In addition, a lack of serious political desire would have to be overcome if the constitution is to be brought into step with the processes and relationships that characterise government and politics in the UK today.

However, in the conclusion to his engaging argument for preserving Britain's traditional constitutional arrangements in a 2006 issue of *Parliamentary Affairs*, Robert Hazell argues that we should embrace our constitution as it is, rather than replace it or — worst of all — neglect it. All citizens should play an active role in nurturing Britain's unique constitutional arrangements since:

> unwritten constitutions can be just as good as written ones…[they] need to be regularly reviewed and updated. They need guardians to protect and defend their underlying values. It is a task that concerns us all…We should nurture our unwritten constitution as a precious part of our heritage; each generation should seek to pass it on to the next.

Box 5.11

Should the UK constitution be codified?

Yes
- The haphazard protection of basic freedoms is unacceptable in a modern democracy.
- The lack of clarity needs to be radically overhauled.
- It is out of keeping with modern democracies, especially EU neighbours.
- Rights would be far better protected within a codified constitution.

No
- The arrangements have served Britain well for many centuries.
- Checks and balances may not be perfect but they do exist and do work.
- Practical problems of codification seem insurmountable.
- Unelected judges will play too large a part in the constitutional arrangements.

Task 5.1

1 What are the advantages of an uncodified constitution?
2 What are the disadvantages of an uncodified constitution?

Guidance

These are the two central questions on the future of the UK's constitutional arrangements and you will need a strong framework in order to answer them effectively. Refer back to where the two questions feature in this chapter. Use a grid on one full side of A4 for each question, with columns for argument, evaluation and examples. In your evaluation, try to make the implications — for democracy and for the protection of rights — of each argument as clear as possible and include at least one illustrative example for each argument.

Task 5.2

Read the extract below and answer the questions which follow.

The long-delayed publication of the Government's Counter-Terrorism Review revealed that control orders will effectively be retained. When the review was announced in June last year, the Home Secretary publicly asked for Liberty's contribution. The human rights group's response explained the problems with the regime and offered alternatives.

The new rebadged system will still include electronic tagging and a residence requirement. Controlees will not be able to meet with certain people or go to certain buildings — although it will be easier for them to use the internet. The control orders will be limited to two years — although if it is possible to make a new order as soon as the existing one expires, then this constraint would be illusory. Crucially, the orders will still be initiated by the Home Secretary — and the regime will continue to run outside the criminal justice system of investigation, arrest, charge and conviction. Both Coalition partners opposed control orders when in opposition.

Shami Chakrabarti, Director of Liberty, said:

'We welcome movement on stop and search, 28-day detention and council snooping, but when it comes to ending punishment without trial; the Government appears to have bottled it. Spin and semantics aside, control orders are retained and rebranded, if in a slightly lower fat form. As before, the innocent may be punished without a fair hearing and the guilty will escape the full force of criminal law. This leaves a familiar bitter taste. Parliament must now decide whether the final flavour will be of progress, disappointment or downright betrayal.'

Source: adapted from the website of Liberty, the civil liberties and human rights group (**www.liberty-human-rights.org.uk**), January 2011

1   Control orders have long been the subject of constitutional debate as they tread the line between individual liberty and national security. Is there ever a case for curtailing someone's freedom without charging him/her or bringing him/her within the normal criminal justice system?

2   How does the lack of a codified constitution impact on the debate over control orders?

Guidance

1   Control orders are used by the government to impose restrictions on people that they suspect pose a terrorist threat but who they do not have enough evidence to prosecute. Think about whether the government should have the power to do this. Start by making a list for and against the use of control orders.

2   Consider how rights are protected under a codified constitution. Look at the arguments within this chapter on rights in the sections for and against codifying the UK's constitutional arrangements.

Further reading

- Bogdanor, V. (2008) 'A codified constitution for Britain?' *Politics Review*, Vol. 18, No. 1.
- Harrison, K. and Boyd, T. (2006) *The Changing Constitution*, Edinburgh University Press.
- www.unlockdemocracy.org.uk
- www.liberty-human-rights.org.uk

The coalition government: a new constitution at last?

The 5 days that it took the Conservative and Liberal Democrat parties to thrash out their historic coalition agreement was exceptionally quick. It would be wrong to suggest that a hung Parliament (and therefore a possible coalition government) was not predicted in the run-up to the 2010 general election. But few — if any — predicted that it would be the Liberal Democrats and Conservatives that would conjoin — forming only the fourth British peacetime coalition in over 100 years.

But the circumstances that surrounded the run-up to the general election itself — record government debt, global economic crisis and a loss of faith in parliamentary politics following the expenses scandal — were extraordinary and became key factors in both the speed of negotiation and the nature of the resulting government itself.

How did constitutional reform provide the basis for the coalition agreement?

For many observers, the biggest irony of the agreement between the Liberal Democrat and Conservative parties remains the prominence of constitutional reform. In both ideology and policy the two parties could hardly be more opposed on the nature, structure and future of Britain's constitution. Yet several interweaving circumstances occurred to turn an unlikely partnership into a viable one. Aside from the grave economic concerns mentioned above, these changing circumstances included:

● The perception that the gap between the Liberal Democrat and Conservative parties had narrowed since the 2005 general election. David Cameron's 'Big Society' reformist agenda had 'liberalised' the Tory Party and shifted the focus of the Conservative Party, allowing for the adoption of policies that were much more geared towards rights, the environment, the accountability of public officials and towards making the functioning of Parliament more responsive and efficient.

- Nick Clegg's personal unpopularity in the wake of the coalition agreement cannot overshadow the way that he had captured the mood of a public that was looking for something fresh and new in the run-up to the general election. Clegg was the impressive 'winner' of the television debates and the Liberal Democrats won a healthy 22% of the vote in the elections. In May 2010, the stature of the Liberal Democrats was at an all-time high — could they really pass up the opportunity of a foothold in power at last?

Constitutional reform: Conservatives versus Liberal Democrats

The Conservative constitutional agenda in early 2010

- For many Conservatives, constitutional reform started and stopped with Britain's membership of the European Union. The relationship between Britain and Europe was viewed with suspicion at best and hostility at worst by the Tory Party rank and file.
- Another key constitutional target for traditional Conservative supporters included the perception of a 'rights culture' created under New Labour. According to some newspapers, hardly a day went by without the further empowerment of criminals, terrorists and illegal immigrants. The replacement of a European-based bill of rights with a British one was seen as a necessary reform (see Box 6.1).
- While generally accepting several of the most important constitutional reforms introduced by New Labour, such as the creation of devolved assemblies, many Conservatives were still uncertain about future reform of the House of Lords.

Box 6.1

David Cameron and the Human Rights Act

When the government introduced the Human Rights Act, it basically imported to British courts lock, stock and barrel the whole European Convention on Human Rights. I think a better solution would be for Britain to write its own Bill of Rights. It would in many ways be similar to the European Convention on Human Rights because bills of rights tend to be quite similar, but it could include a better explanation of rights and responsibilities, it could include clearer definitions, it could include some particularly British rights that we feel strongly about, like jury trial, and I think it would be better to have that in British courts.

Source: D. Cameron and D. Jones, *Cameron on Cameron: conversations with Dylan Jones* (2008)

The Liberal Democrat constitutional agenda in 2010

- Unlike the Conservative Party, the profile of constitutional reform within Liberal Democrat ranks had always been high. The Liberal Democrats had pushed for devolution, the entrenchment of basic rights and reforms to the functioning of the Westminster assembly far earlier than the Labour Party had.
- In the run-up to several 'turning-point' elections — particularly 1992, 1997 and 2005 — it was clear that a commitment to major constitutional reform would be the basis of any coalition agreement that involved the Liberal Democrats. The 2010 election was no different and the Liberal Democrat focus on electoral reform, the protection of rights and the placing of limits on executive power was unswerving.
- The prospect of a coalition agreement with the Labour Party — Brown's administration had stalled on almost every aspect of proposed constitutional changes — became far less appealing than one with the Conservatives. David Cameron had made clear pledges on the future functioning of Parliament and had placed two causes dear to Liberal Democrat hearts — the environment and rights — at the forefront of proposals for constitutional change.

Box 6.2

Nick Clegg on government power

'I need to say this — you shouldn't trust any government, actually including this one. You should not trust government — full stop. The natural inclination of government is to hoard power and information; to accrue power to itself in the name of the public good.'

Source: quoted in H. Porter, 'Why we should believe Nick Clegg when he promises to restore liberties stolen by Labour', *Guardian*, February 2011

While specific disagreement occurred over tuition fees (which may threaten Liberal Democrat MPs for several years to come) certain key constitutional reforms — Trident, taxation issues and attitudes to law and order — provided fertile ground on which to hatch the coalition.

- Electoral reform was seen as a prime area of 'coalition compromise', with the proposal of a referendum on reforming the electoral system used for Westminster elections. While many Conservatives looked set to oppose it and many Liberal Democrats saw the alternative vote as the most disappointing of all electoral alternatives to first-past-the-post, the decision was put in the hands of the electorate.

- In addition, the area of rights looked set for a substantial overhaul. David Cameron had long been pushing for a British Bill of Rights though this would not, disappointingly for the Liberal Democrats, become an over-arching document set to replace the principle of parliamentary sovereignty.

What are the constitutional implications of the coalition government itself?

Nick Clegg and David Cameron during a joint press conference in the Downing Street garden following the announcement of their historic coalition agreement

The strengths and weaknesses of coalition governments had been well rehearsed prior to 2010. Coalitions, it is said, lack legitimacy, with policies being the product of compromises between two or more parties. Pledges, promises and principles are sacrificed in the name of pragmatism. As Rob Wilson explains in *5 Days to Power*, which casts an insider look at the days that forged the coalition government in the UK:

Few of the electorate actively sought a coalition government. Many indeed believed that such a government would be weak, unstable and incapable of dealing with the country's massive economic problems. The Conservative campaign had played on the fear that a hung parliament (that is, a parliament in which no single party holds an overall majority of seats) would be destabilising and damaging for the country.

Manifesto differences

Even a quick glance at the manifesto commitments of the two parties concerning constitutional reform in the run-up to the 2010 general election reveals differences on a scale that contributed to the near certainty that any post-election coalition would not be between the Conservatives and the Liberal Democrats:

- Where the Conservatives were committed to replacing the Human Rights Act (with a British Bill of Rights) the Liberal Democrats were committed to protecting it.
- While the Liberal Democrats affirmed their commitment to proportional representation for elections to Westminster, the Conservatives were staunch supporters of first-past-the-post.
- The Conservative Party's hesitancy over the form and composition of a second chamber was in marked contrast to the Liberal Democrat assertion that a fully elected second chamber was the only way forward for the Lords.
- Other key Liberal Democrat pledges — on fixed-term parliaments and on lowering the voting age to 16 — were not mentioned by the Conservatives.

Questions of legitimacy

The above differences were just in the area of constitutional reform. There were also stark differences over Trident, tuition fees and cutting the deficit. Small wonder, say many commentators, that questions of legitimacy surround the coalition government. Vernon Bogdanor identifies two key issues that face the coalition government in its infancy, suggesting that:

> for a start, the government faces real pressures to justify its legitimacy in response to cries that no one voted for it. Second, British electoral laws and principles of cabinet government must adapt even further to the deep social changes occurring in this country. Can the coalition deliver this?

A response to the first 'pressure' will not come before the next election, but several significant Tories — including John Major in his Churchill lecture at

Cambridge in November 2010 — are already suggesting that the next election must be fought by the two parties together. The practical reality of constituency parties withdrawing their own candidates in favour of one from another party may provoke strong local reactions.

With just three peacetime coalitions in well over a century there is hardly a wealth of evidence to base assumptions on when considering the current one. But one clear disparity between the government of Cameron and Clegg and former coalitions lies in the fact that while the three previous agreements were forged before an election and endorsed categorically by it, the current prime minister's pre-election dark warnings of decisions being taken 'behind closed doors' and 'instead of policies implemented on the basis of a manifesto there will be compromises and half-measures' were borne out by events.

Prime ministerial power in a coalition government

In addition, the traditional constitutional power of a prime minister to appoint and dismiss a minister is blurred by the existence of ministers who are in his government but not in his party. How far the doctrine of individual ministerial responsibility will be allowed to stretch if there is disagreement between David Cameron and Nick Clegg over a wayward minister is open to debate, but what is clear is that there has been a significant shift in the ability of a prime minister to act decisively in this area.

What are the prospects for a 'new constitution' under the coalition government?

One cannot divorce the creation of the coalition government from the environment that gave rise to it. The motives behind the deal that was struck on 10 May 2010 between Cameron and Clegg, and which formed the coalition government, ranged from the pragmatic (without Liberal Democrat support, Cameron's short-term parliamentary prospects were slim) to the ideological, since there is no doubt that the two leaders shared a genuine reformist agenda.

May to July 2010: reshaping the constitutional landscape

Several significant documents emerged from the coalition government in the first 100 days of its existence. Although each of them covered disparate aspects of policy and government strategy there was a distinct flavour of constitutional reform to bind them.

The Coalition: Our Programme for Government

On 20 May 2010 the government published its first document. It was effectively a joint manifesto to make up for the glaring lack of one during the campaign itself. It was also the product of several weeks of frenetic negotiation and compromise between the key figures in both parties. The 34-page document set out far-reaching plans that would affect many areas from families to foreign affairs and from taxation to transport, including:

- On **civil liberties** the document made explicit commitments to restoring rights and freedoms and limited state power in areas such as ID cards, the DNA database and CCTV surveillance.
- On **decentralisation**, the document was emphatic that there would be a fundamental shift of power from Westminster to the people and far greater democratic engagement: 'we will end the era of top-down government by giving new powers to local councils, communities, neighbourhoods and individuals'.
- In terms of **transparency** of government, the coalition government referred to the 'need to throw open the doors of public bodies, to enable the public to hold politicians and public bodies to account'. The emphasis was clearly on deficit reduction but also on 'setting government data free'.

Box 6.3

The Coalition: Our Programme for Government on civil liberties

We will be strong in defence of freedom. The Government believes that the British state has become too authoritarian, and that over the past decade it has abused and eroded fundamental human freedoms and historic civil liberties. We need to restore the rights of individuals in the face of encroaching state power, in keeping with Britain's tradition of freedom and fairness.

Source: *The Coalition: Our Programme for Government* (2010)

This first coalition statement of intent covered plans for the future of the Post Office, substantial cuts to non-frontline public services and the announcement of a full spending review in the autumn. Cameron and Clegg were united in its potential. To the prime minister it represented 'a full and comprehensive reform agenda'; his deputy claimed that 'you've never read a document like this'.

Agreement for Stability and Reform

The next series of publications came just a day later on 21 May 2010 and comprised three separate documents. They revolved around:

- a new ministerial code, barring ministers from lobbying government for 2 years, placing restrictions on advisers and government cars and requiring regular publication of ministerial meetings
- a committee list showing a reduction in the number of committees and listing the members of each, including the chairs and deputy chairs which in each case will include a member from both the coalition partners
- the setting out of the practical operational arrangements for how the coalition will operate

Box 6.4

Agreement for Stability and Reform: explanation of the government structure from the cabinet office

The Prime Minister is responsible for the overall organisation of the executive and the allocation of functions between ministers in charge of ministerial departments. In general, the ministerial head of a department — usually a secretary of state — has responsibility for a set of policy issues and associated legislation, and these responsibilities are delivered through their department and its delivery partners.

In addition to ministerial departments there are non-ministerial departments and executive agencies. Agencies carry out some of the executive functions of government and are part of a government department, but have their own management and budget.

The responsibilities of ministers and the structure of government are kept under review to ensure fitness for purpose. As the challenges the country faces and the Government's priorities change, the Prime Minister may wish to reorganise the roles of Cabinet ministers and the Government. This could involve a combination of reallocating responsibilities between ministers, creating a new department or renaming departments. This is referred to as a machinery of government change.

Source: adapted from the Cabinet Office website (**www.cabinetoffice.gov.uk**)

This document (see Box 6.4) provided a higher degree of clarity than ever before on the role of the prime minister in relation to ministers, departments and executive agencies. Under a coalition government, such a level of clarity is especially necessary, but it also further codifies the previously unofficial nature of the relationship between a prime minister and his or her cabinet.

Political Reform Draft Structural Reform Plan

The third document — the *Political Reform Draft Structural Reform Plan* — was the clearest of all the documents to identify constitutional concerns and goals for reform. It made specific reference to 'the over-concentration of power in an over-centralised state'; the 'authoritarian' nature of the UK state and an affirmation that 'to restore the balance we need to redistribute power and accountability back where it belongs, restore civil liberties and promote the autonomy of the self-determination of the individual and the neighbourhood'.

It was this document that provided clarity for the coalition government's constitutional agenda and a future path for reform. In constitutional terms it referred to:

- a commitment to electoral reform
- open primaries and recall elections for MPs
- reforms to the functioning of the Commons and the composition of the Lords
- reforms to the powers of the Welsh Assembly
- a Freedom Bill and a British Bill of Rights

In the next few months greater clarity was given to several key areas.

The coalition government and parliamentary reform

The **Fixed-term Parliaments Bill** presents an interesting angle on reform. Nick Clegg outlined its 'revolutionary' potential, explaining in Parliament that 'by setting the date that Parliament will dissolve, our prime minister is giving up the right to pick and choose the date of the next general election—that's a true first in British politics.' An amendment insisting on 4-year, rather than 5-year, fixed terms, backed by Labour and the nationalist parties, was defeated in November 2010.

But rather than enhance democracy, some commentators assert that fixed-term parliaments present smaller coalition partners with regular opportunities to make or break their coalitions without fear of immediate electoral consequences. In addition, part of the change involves the requirement that

55% of the House (rather than a simple majority) are needed to dissolve the House on a vote of no confidence.

Box 6.5

Lord Cormack and the second reading of the Fixed-term Parliament Bill, March 2011

An advocate of the merits of fixed-term parliaments in the past, Lord Cormack said that 'as always, the devil is in the detail.'

The 'logical case' for fixing the term had been often rehearsed: 'we remove the manipulative power of the Prime Minister of the day, we create a symmetry with other parliamentary, assembly and local government elections and we become similar to many other democracies,' he said. It was, nevertheless, essential 'not to deprive the elected House of the power to turf out' a Government that had lost its confidence. 'The Bill before us recognises this, but only up to a point.' Recounting the vote of 'no confidence' in the 1979 Labour Government, Lord Cormack said that 'under the terms of this Bill as it stands, that vote in itself would not have triggered an immediate general election.'

Source: **www.parliament.uk**

The House of Commons

In the wake of the expenses scandal, reform of many aspects of the functioning of the Commons was an area that all parties were ready to push for in 2010. The Wright Committee on Reform to the House of Commons (2009) had made many clear statements on the 'beefing up' of backbench power, the majority of which had been accepted. The coalition government committed to implementing all of the committee's proposed reforms, including the setting up of a Backbench Business Committee which was to have more 'say' over the parliamentary agenda.

In addition, recall elections (of errant MPs accused of infringing parliamentary rules) were supported by both parties in their 2010 manifestos and the potential for real reform in this area looks strong.

The House of Lords

The coalition government agreed to create a committee to begin the drafting of proposals for the future of the Lords — on elected or partially elected grounds. While there is commitment to addressing the party imbalance in the Lords, prospects for definitive reform are uncertain since divisions over the chamber's future are not just along party lines.

The coalition government and electoral reform

The immediate prospects for electoral reform — itself a central plank in the original agreement — were determined at the May 2011 referendum. But although the alternative vote was rejected, with an emphatic 70/30 split against, the issue will not go away for the Liberal Democrats. Any reform to make the electoral system more representative (if not more proportional) would have significant benefits for the Liberal Democrat party since the party is the natural 'second choice' among Labour and Conservative supporters alike.

The alternative vote would also have removed the divisive prospect of constituency parties having to withdraw candidates to allow their coalition partner's candidate a 'free ride'. However, the historic resistance of the Conservative Party to a reform that would necessarily disadvantage it was maintained.

The coalition government and civil rights

In a *Guardian* article published on 13 February 2011 entitled 'Why we should believe Nick Clegg when he promises to restore liberties stolen by Labour' Henry Porter referred to a number of successes that the Liberal Democrats had enjoyed as members of the coalition government. Nick Clegg's 'own firm belief in individual liberty has been placed at the heart of the coalition's programme' said Porter. This feature rapidly bore fruit in the form of the Protection of Freedoms Bill. Clegg himself maintained that he was 'amazed how far we pushed the whole security establishment and the Home Office in a liberal direction'.

Box 6.6

Key aspects of the Protection of Freedoms Bill

- An end to ID cards
- An end to the national children's database
- Removing police stop and search powers
- Controlling the use of surveillance by councils
- A reduction in pre-charge detention for terrorist suspects to 14 days (at the end of Blair's prime ministership, Blair himself called for 90 days)
- The protection of jury trial
- The extension and strengthening of the Freedom of Information Act

The coalition agreement saw the disappearance of several notable pre-election pledges, one of them being the almost immediate replacement of the Human Rights Act with a much-watered-down British version, made — and subsequently abandoned — by the Conservatives. However, the creation of a commission to investigate the case for a British Bill of Rights was a notable Liberal Democrat success (see Box 6.7).

Box 6.7

The British Bill of Rights Commission

On 18 March 2011 the coalition government launched a commission to investigate the case for a British Bill of Rights. The creation of the commission was a key pledge in the coalition agreement and represents a major goal of the Liberal Democrat Party. It has also been welcomed by Conservative critics of the Human Rights Act.

The terms of the commission are clear that there will be no withdrawal from legislation incorporating the ECHR into British domestic law. Instead the commission is charged with creating a bill of rights that 'incorporates and builds on all our obligations under the European Convention on Human Rights, ensures that these rights continue to be enshrined in UK law, and protects and extends our liberties.'

It will publish an interim report prior to its final report by the end of 2012.

There is much speculation about how the commission will function with some commentators suggesting that it will be 'deadlocked from the start'. The deputy prime minister Nick Clegg has found that enthusiastic supporters of human rights are counter-balanced by more sceptical voices selected by justice secretary Kenneth Clarke, some of whom have argued for Britain's withdrawal from the European Convention on Human Rights.

The coalition government and devolution

Such has been the success of the devolution project that it hardly seems possible that the issue could once have been so conspicuous in providing 'clear blue water' between the parties in the 1990s. By 2010, Conservative fears over the fragmentation of the UK had given way to an acknowledgment of the pragmatic basis to the power-sharing structure. Proposals to devolve more power to local and regional level — in particular in the areas of health, education, social services and housing — appear to echo Liberal Democrat commitments to local communities.

The coalition government and Europe

The issue of Britain's relationship with Europe has long dogged the Conservative Party and the fact that the two parties — arguably on polar opposites of the euro-spectrum — could reach agreement on this subject was particularly surprising. However, in the years prior to 2010 there had been shifts in both parties on 'Europe', each one inching towards the centre ground. Certain commitments appeared to pacify both parties:

- joining, or preparing to join, the euro in the life of the Parliament was ruled out
- the commitment to put to a referendum any further treaty that threatened to transfer sovereignty to Europe was made
- the potential for a UK sovereignty bill was articulated, which would emphasise the ultimate sovereignty of the UK Parliament

Conclusion

If one considers the opening statement to Rob Wilson's account of the *5 Days to Power* (2010) to be true — that the forming of the coalition government was 'a simple and raw fight for the ultimate prize in political power that the country can bestow: the office of Prime Minister' — then the compromises that took place as a consequence can only be viewed in this light.

The ease with which commitments and principles were shelved in the desire to form a working government is, at times, remarkable. Our focus though, has been on constitutional reform — rather than deficit reduction, law and order or other key areas of policy — and in this sphere perhaps like no other, the Liberal Democrat push for a referendum on electoral reform, the protection of the Human Rights Act and a commitment to local government has been significant.

But the issues of a new constitution run wider and deeper than this. The British constitution cannot be separated from British society, and that society has changed profoundly from the partisan-aligned, two-party, homogenous state that existed until the 1960s.

British people live longer; they have more leisure time and more disposable income. Society is more individualistic and fragmented, multicultural and multifaith. Modern politics is about choice, diversity and aspiration and not about a one-size-fits-all unitary state.

But modern politics also needs to become more responsive. For instance, proposals for open primaries to determine candidate selection, for recall elections to hold errant MPs to account and for referendums to determine key policies, all reflect accurately the public mood for change. A new constitution is not merely about the composition of the Lords or Britain's relationship with Europe. It is about a framework that reflects a new age appropriately — one that is properly and finally characterised by the sovereignty of the people.

Task 6.1

1 What are the main concerns about the constitutional position of the coalition government?

2 How might these concerns be resolved?

Guidance

1 Look back to the second question of this chapter. Why are there doubts over the legitimacy of the coalition government?

2 In the same section there are suggestions to overcome these concerns. What are they?

Task 6.2

Read the extract below and answer the questions which follow.

Sir Gus O'Donnell on the Cabinet Manual: 'More than just a Janet & John guide to the Queen and stuff'

Published by the Cabinet Office, a draft version of the Cabinet Manual is currently being considered by three parliamentary select committees while a consultation period is scheduled to end on 8 March.

Sir Gus explained that the Manual is intended to 'help the public better understand how our democracy works' by making the inner workings of government more transparent. He emphasised, however, that it is not intended to be an exhaustive description of existing practices: rather, the Manual should act as a 'high-level summary' of areas such as ministerial responsibility, devolution and hung parliaments. Sir Gus also took time to address some criticisms that have been directed at the Cabinet Manual as well as some myths that surround it.

It is not, he stated, a written constitution with a defined legal status, nor is it intended to direct the administration of government. It is a statement of how the executive functions and one that is written in an understandable manner: no Erskine May or Magna Carta but a 'work of reference that guides those of us who work in or with

Task 6.2 (continued)

government, and opens up how government works so that it can be better understood by people across the country.'

In February 2010 the skeleton structure of the Manual as well as a draft chapter on elections and government formation were published. This draft was to take practical effect after the May 2010 general election. Sir Gus argued that the Manual served as a 'useful, modest piece of guidance' during the political negotiations which immediately followed.

Furthermore he rejected criticisms that publication of the draft chapter had unduly influenced those negotiations: whether that was by dictating the speed at which negotiations between the Conservatives and Liberal Democrats should take place or for how long Prime Minister Gordon Brown should stay in office.

Sir Gus contended that the most fundamental conclusion to be drawn from those 'five days in May' is that the civil service was fully able to meet the challenge presented by this 'unusual situation'.

Sir Gus concluded his presentation by reiterating that the Cabinet Manual should not be understood as a seminal constitutional document but, nevertheless, should act as more than, in the words of Lord Powell, 'a bit of a Janet and John guide to the Queen and so on'.

> Source: adapted from a report by Patrick Graham on the UCL Constitution Unit website (**www.ucl.ac.uk/constitution-unit**) on the address delivered by Sir Gus O'Donnell (cabinet secretary, head of the civil service and permanent secretary of the cabinet office) on 24 February 2011 at the Institute for Government

1   The Cabinet Manual has attracted some criticism. Use the extract to summarise what Sir Gus O'Donnell suggests that the Manual represents.
2   Why was Sir Gus forced to reject criticisms that the draft unduly influenced the negotiation process that led to the coalition government?

Guidance

1   Do some research on the Cabinet Manual produced by Sir Gus O'Donnell. Type 'Gus O'Donnell Cabinet Manual' into an internet search engine and see what you can find out. Look particularly for comment and opinion on how the Cabinet Manual featured in the '5 days' that saw power handed from a Labour government to a coalition of Conservative and Liberal Democrat parties. One good place to start might be the Constitution Unit of UCL itself: **www.ucl.ac.uk/constitution-unit**
2   In order to answer why Sir Gus was forced to reject these criticisms you will need to have made some notes on why the criticisms were forwarded in the first place.

Further reading

- Bogdanor, V. (2011) 'This is only the start', *Prospect Magazine*.
- Fairclough, P., McNaughton, N. and Magee, E. (2011) *UK Government and Politics Annual Survey 2011*, Philip Allan Updates.
- Stoten, D. W. (2011) 'The coalition government and constitutional reform', *Politics Review*, Vol. 20, No. 3.
- Wilson, R. (2010) *5 Days to Power*, Biteback Publishing.

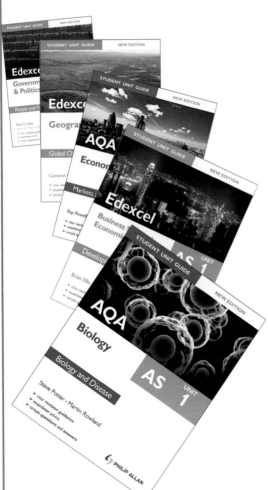

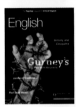
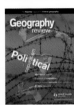